EMOTIONAL PAIN

VERSUS

SUICIDE

&

(EMOTIONAL BLINDNESS)

BY

M. Kukreja, M.D.

EMOTIONAL PAIN

VERSUS

SUICIDE

&

(EMOTIONAL BLINDNESS)

By

M. Kukreja, M.D.

Please note that this book only uses the word "he" for convenience. Everything applies equally, as far as possible, to men and women.

THINK ABOUT THIS.

If someone has rejected you, why are you rejecting yourself?

If others have caused you pain, why are you causing pain to yourself?

If others are causing you pain, how can they be considered yours?

Never disrespect an item or religion that another person values. This is one of the greatest causes of emotional pain.

Feeling sorry for yourself loses the enthusiasm for life.

We have forgotten that the purpose of education should always be first Moral Rules, then character, then "How to Handle Bad Times," and only then, the knowledge of the outside world."

The result is the present moral chaos and emotional pain as children murder their parents, teachers, and other students.

Did you teach your child right from wrong or self-control?

"To educate a man in the mind, but not in morals, is to educate a menace to society."

President Theodore Roosevelt

LIVING IN ONE HOME

Our judges are guilty of causing severe emotional pain to countless innocent children under the pretext of "being fair."

They do not understand that living in **"one and the same home"** leads to a stable personality, be it an orphan or a child from a divorced home.

By bending backward to be fair to both parents, judges have completely destroyed the development and welfare of a child.

Perhaps the judges should shift their homes every week. Let them try it for a year.

Even a plant cannot live if you uproot it every week.

How did you think of doing this to a human?

It is criminal and non-caring to keep shifting a child through different foster homes or from one parent to another. At least the orphanage keeps a child in one stable place. Why is it that the rest of the world understands this?

Foster homes must be banned!

CONTENTS

Emotional pain is worse than physical pain.

Sometimes it leads to suicide.

That is why both topics are discussed in this book.

PREFACE

Emotional pain is as severe as physical pain. It makes us stop living "normal lives." It removes our ability to enjoy life or fulfill our potential and talents. It prevents us from being productive individuals and ruins our intelligence. As a result, we can no longer make intelligent decisions concerning our welfare or that of others.

It can lead us to destroy our lives or the lives of others around us. In its extreme throes, we no longer want to live.

The following are unanswered questions.

1. How we deal with this pain has been left entirely to chance and on our whims! Why?

2. How do you approach a person in severe emotional pain or heading toward suicide?

3. When Should You Teach "A Protocol for Bad Times?"

It is essential to know that emotions follow definite rules, too.

This book wants to approach a person not only while he is thrashing in pain but hopefully before as well. It is best if he reads it when he is not affected. Then, he would be calm enough to grasp its contents and form his plan.

Perhaps the book is being looked at by someone so overcome with emotional pain that he cannot think straight. That is okay. A seed may be planted. He may return to it later when he vaguely remembers that something helpful might have been written here.

The author has introduced several new terms, "Emotional Blindness" is one such term. We go about our daily activities, oblivious to what is happening in front of us until it is too late, and we are left devasted. We must regularly check "The Pulse of our Family Life." We must also have an "Emotional Boundary" and a Moral Boundary.

Other programs have been introduced. There are "The S.T.O.P. Program" and "The Seven-Step Program" to deal with emotional pain. Finally, the author encourages the reader to implement the chapter "Handle the Pain," with its stages, before he leaves this world.

M. Kukreja, M.D.

PART 1: EMOTIONAL PAIN

CHAPTER 1: WHY WAS I BORN?

When we are in terrible emotional pain, it helps us to remember why we were born. We have not come into this world by accident.

Each of us has been sent here with a purpose.

We have come here to climb the long staircase of development. We each have arrived at a different step, but we will be sent here again and again until we reach the highest step.

You came here to develop. Whether you do or not is entirely up to you.

Suppose you were on earth in the third grade. You decided that you did not want to go to school. You did not like it. Guess what your parents will do? Send you right back!   Similarly, if you leave the Earth, you will be *sent right back* until you learn your lesson. The Earth is your school.

One may have been sent here to overcome his selfishness, while another to develop courage. A third person may be sent to learn to control his emotions. You are to first do the " prerequisite courses," and then are faced with your challenge or weakness. Whether you pass or not is entirely up to you.

Or, you may have already graduated but have been sent here to help another person who is struggling with his lesson. Or, you may be sent here to teach someone.

You are not allowed to refuse. You already agreed to it in your contract before.

But understand that to teach or help another being, you still have to go through some scenarios, however painful they may be, to fine-tune you.

Since you will be sent back again, why not develop in the first round? A lot of time was spent in the other world to prepare for your journey in this life. Why waste it?

Your job is to do the best you can with the knowledge you have and the circumstances that you are in.

Having self-value and self-worth is critical.

Your Creator does not send any worthless being to this earth. Did you know that? So why do you think that you do not have self-worth? Check to see what gifts you possess. One of them is intelligence. You are an intelligent being. But intelligence has nothing to do with academic degrees.

Intelligence is the ability to find a solution to a problem or to work around it.

If you have a problem, use your intelligence, not your emotions, to explore your alternatives. Value time.

Give yourself one year to see what happens.

But development is beyond intelligence.

Personal development means self-control and self-discipline, following a moral map, having a high value for yourself, and having love, compassion, and fairness toward others.

Can you comfort someone, give them love, make them feel safe, and make them laugh? Can you be a good friend? Can you earn enough to save money to help someone else? Are you able to give shelter to an animal that would die otherwise or provide a home to an orphan? You are on the right path if even two of these aspects are fine.

But this is how you treat others. What about your personal development?

That is described in detail elsewhere. But for now, know that you cannot develop as long as you do not value yourself, do not have self-worth, do not have self-control, are angry, rude, insulting, insensitive to others, selfish, cruel, greedy, and have the seven cardinal sins.

CHAPTER 2: THE EFFECTS OF EMOTIONAL PAIN

The following are some of the effects of emotional pain:

Premature aging.

Destruction of our physical and mental health.

Illnesses.

Fatal autoimmune disorders.

Loss of teeth.

Depression.

Turning into a bitter and angry person.

The tendency toward accidents.

Homicides and Suicide.

Instead of protecting ourselves and our welfare, we become our worst enemies.

CHAPTER 3: WHEN SHOULD YOU TEACH?

When Should You Teach "A Protocol for Bad Times?"

The "protocol" should be taught **before** bad times happen, preferably by the age of twelve.

First, the child needs to learn this to advance his development.

Second, you cannot teach this *later* to someone who now thinks that he knows everything.

Third, this cannot be taught during bad times. One cannot process new ideas when one is involved in a situation,

However, one will fall back on what one already knows.

Fourth, intense emotions, whether sorrow, emotional pain, shock, anger, hatred, or depression, cover one like a thick blanket. Suggestions simply cannot penetrate.

A parent's duty is to build his children's character before building their muscles. In character, one must teach children how to face good and bad times. It becomes tragic when a parent does not do so.

CHAPTER 4: DESPITE THE PAIN

Here are examples of some people who rose from pain and suffering. They went on to make their lives, and of those around them, better.

Hellen Keller was blind and deaf but wrote a book and led an inspiring life.

Jay-Z was from an impoverished neighborhood.

Beethoven wrote concerts, though he was deaf.

Thomas Edison failed over a hundred times before he invented the light bulb that lights your room.

President Franklin Roosevelt, one of the greatest presidents of the United States, was paralyzed by Polio. He was the only president to be elected four times.

Oprah Winfrey was poor, raped, and delivered a child at the age of fourteen.

Ralph Lauren is a fashion designer who grew up as a poor immigrant in the Bronx.

Dolly Parton was raised in a one-room cabin with dirt floors

J.K. Rowling, the author of Harry Potter, was so poor that she spent nights not eating so that her child could eat

Nelson Mandela spent 27 years in prison (not knowing if he would be killed the next day) and went on to free his country.

Stephen Hawkins was paralyzed in all four limbs, but he was one of the most intelligent scientists and taught us about black holes in space.

Viktor Frankl survived four years in a brutal Nazi concentration camp where he underwent torture. On being released, he found his whole family destroyed. However, he rebuilt his life, became a psychiatrist, and wrote many books. His book, entitled "The Search for Meaning," states that individuals are able to endure hardships if they can dedicate their suffering to a greater cause.

Tesla dug ditches to survive.

PART 2: ACUTE EMOTIONAL PAIN

CHAPTER 5: RULES IN ACUTE PAIN

In acute pain, the following rules apply:

Violence is not an option.

Do not destroy property.

Do not destroy another person.

Do not destroy yourself.

Never think that if you cannot have a person, someone else should not have him, either.

A person is not an object. He has a right to live. He has been sent to this earth for a purpose unique to him.

If a person you love prefers another, let him go. True love submits to the happiness of the one he loves.

If you have lost your children in a divorce, do not kill them. Love them from afar, if necessary. Be there in time of need. But always be fair and respectful to the other parent.

There is no greater crime than killing your children. Your pain does not justify this.

What if you had invested money and emotions over a long period? It was a long marriage, and now your spouse is unfaithful. Your children, over whom you spent sleepless nights, now chose the other parent who was hardly at home.

You are going through so much. You have had a loss. In this relationship, your trust has been betrayed. Add to this your loneliness, the pain of rejection, and the desperate longing for things to return to how they were.

You have lost yourself. Your self-value, self-worth, and self-confidence have been severely jolted, and you have to regain them. You have been shattered into a thousand pieces.

How do you put them together again? What do you do? How do you go on?

First comes the "Pause."

CHAPTER 6: FIRST, THE PAUSE

We have good and bad emotions. Compassion is a good emotion, while hatred is a destructive emotion.

Bad emotions always want you to carry out their orders immediately. This is because they are afraid you may change your mind.

So, they will urge you to "Kill NOW! Rape NOW! Attack NOW! Destroy or break things NOW!

But if you pause and think instead of acting, it may prevent you from doing what you will later regret or destroying your life, as in going to jail.

The Pause is critical!

Your emotions will never tell you to do *"good deeds now"*. It is because these emotions are not interested in good deeds.

Are you going to let your feelings be your masters?

Are you going to be a puppet controlled by your feelings?

Or are you going to show that your mind is in charge?

Do you have the willpower?

We start with the pause.

Rules of the Pause:

No decision. No action.

Violence is not an option.

We do not destroy property.

We do not kill another person.

We do not kill ourselves.

When you first hear bad news, the following sequence should occur.

1. You are in shock: "What did I hear/see?"   Your core is thrown off balance.

2. PAUSE (The pause is not empty). See below as to what you are doing in this pause).

3. Next, you must bring your core back to a *steady state*. What does the "steady state" mean? Be in charge. Be in control. Count to ten slowly. Control your breathing. Make it slow. Become calm.

   There must be no anger. Anger makes a person stupid. He is unable to think correctly or make the right decision.

   You cannot speak in this state because in speaking you will lose this control.

   If you focus on your current emotion, it will become stronger. So, you must distract yourself.

   Think of yourself as a very calm person.

4. Come to a decision. You can postpone your decision and walk away saying you will come back to this later.

5. **There must be no revenge in this decision.**

6. Then "speak, act, or both."

The pause is not empty. Pause means to be silent. *Say nothing and do nothing.* But you should **be thinking** of the following things during this pause:

A. Remember the rules of the pause.

B. Think about the intent of the other person.

C. What are the consequences to me and others? How do I survive?

D. What is the moral thing for me to do?

If you continue to speak, fight back, or repeat yourself, you lose the respect of others, and you cannot think clearly about the right action to take. You need silence to think clearly.

When the tongue is moving, the mind cannot think!

CHAPTER 7: HANDLE ACUTE PAIN

After the pause, we do the following.

Time

Give yourself time to recover. Start with thirty days.

Start with one day at a time.

Take time to go through this pain. This is not the time to work.

Purpose

Right now, your purpose is to get through this pain. This scenario is given to you perhaps to develop your courage.

Stages

Go through the stages of roll, deal, and heal from the pain. See the chapters ahead in Part 5, "Handle the pain."

Steady Your Inner Core

At the same time as you are doing the above, you must steady your inner self. Your "inner core" has been thrown off balance by the sudden, unexpected events. It is not only in shock but loses its will to function and protect itself.

There are certain steps for this.

Take care of yourself.

Dilute your pain

Recover what you lost.

Throw away your deficiencies

Value

Learn two lessons

Learn about emotions

Pray

Philosophy

Start by asking one question. Why have you narrowed your circle? There are billions of people in the world. Why would you give power to one or four people to influence you not to live? Is that fair to others that you would have otherwise come across?

Take care of yourself.

Start by taking care of yourself, especially since you do not want to, especially when you would rather lie down and die. Take care of yourself as you would of your child.

When did you really take care of yourself.? You were too busy taking care of others. **Why does a soldier go through the daily routine of taking care of his belongings?** He is going to die anyway. It is because it makes him disciplined and, therefore stronger inside.

Taking care of yourself means that you take charge of your life. Do not live to please others.

Dilute your pain

Dilute your pain by talking to friends and strangers and playing with animals.

Your pain does not justify your giving pain to others.

Recover yourself

Somewhere, you lost your self-value, self-worth, and self-confidence. You need to find them.

Show your self-worth in how you dress and the appearance of your surroundings. Your self-worth was not destroyed by this act, betrayal, rejection, or loss. Look at all you had achieved in knowledge and friendships before you met the current people or before this event happened. Did they not consider you valuable? Did you not survive before you met your current loved ones?

Do not lose your self-respect. Protect it at all times.

What about your self-confidence? What makes you think you cannot rise from your ashes?

What makes you think you cannot rebuild your life?

You can handle it!

Throw away your deficiencies.

Throw away your running after others for their love.

Throw away your "disease to please."

Throw away your fear of failure.

Value

Value your work and money. They are part of who you are. They will sustain you when you have nothing left.

Learn two lessons

Acceptance that this is part of life or destiny is vital. Acceptance makes us free to live again.

Learn to let go of who and what want to go, or has gone.

Learn about emotions

Learn about the rules of emotions.

Pray

Pray for inner strength.

Philosophy

They are who they are.

It is what it is.

This is part of my destiny.

Suicide is not a choice right now. I survived before these people came into my life, and I can somehow survive now.

Your chances and duration of recovery are in direct proportion to your self-worth and philosophy.

CHAPTER 8: A LETTER TO YOU

(There is a separate letter directed to the youth in chapter 45 in the second part of this book).

Dear loved one,

Do you see life as steady, grey, heavy, and unbearable? Are you too depressed to live? Or, have you been suddenly hit by situations and are in shock? For example, is there a natural disaster, an earthquake, or a collapsed building?

Then there are acts by others. Perhaps you have been betrayed. Your spouse has left you. You failed or were rejected in an interview. You were assaulted. The gunman walked into a school and killed your children. You have suffered an unbearable loss. The loss of a child is extremely painful. How can anyone recover?

What if you have no one to call your own?

Perhaps you have the daily pain of abuse. Your relationship may be causing tremendous pain.

And what about the pain of a child who is given up for adoption?

It is the ultimate rejection of a helpless being!

There is no concern for what the child will go through in life from no fault of his own. He may be assaulted and abused and suffer extreme emotional pain, abuse, or neglect. Later, the parent will tell such a child on meeting him that she "always loved him." That is not true. Love is shown in actions, not in words.

She is responsible for his pain! No animal will abandon its young! A parent who loves his child will go through hell and fire to keep the child, nourish, protect, and raise him.

Love means to protect.

One is also doomed to a life of pain if one has an inferiority complex, dependency (cannot let go), has "a disease to please," or is running after people for their love.

Life will be painful if one lacks self-respect, and has no value for work or money.

Life will be painful if one has a "false nobility" based on self-sacrifice and protecting an abuser.

The above paragraphs create a complete cocktail of suffering! But you did not even know you had these deficiencies. No one taught you to be aware of your character!

Life will also be painful if you live with one who is greedy, immoral, abusive, has an addiction to power, wants to control others, or is lazy and shirks responsibilities. Do you have the courage to leave him? Do you recognize abuse?

People who say that you should "build a wall" around you through which the abuser's words cannot reach you have no idea what they are talking about.

No such wall can be built as long as there are daily interactions. The interactions poke holes in the wall in an already wounded person. Only when you have been completely separated from an abuser for a year or two and have healed, can you build a wall where his words can no longer hurt!

You have shattered into a thousand pieces. How do you put yourself together? How do you will yourself to go on keeping your sanity intact? How do you rebuild your life, which is in shambles right now? You do not even want to do that! Where do you see the light in the darkness of ignorance and despair?

Your question is, "How do I live?"

Frankel pointed out in his book that a man must have a "why to live" in order to have a "how to live." If you have minors or parents, your duty is clear. You must be around to help them. Even if your children have left you, the other parent may die or become bankrupt.

Here is a person who is broken, in the throes of despair, and disinterested in life.

How do you help him reach a stage where he accepts his pain but can live with it and where he values himself as much as another?

How do you make him calm, confident, curious, peaceful, strong, and happy again?

This book guides you down the path. Recovery is a painful process. The book addresses how to deal with and heal from pain and the associated emotions. It divides the stages you go through to recover and how to get stronger. It helps you to see the facts about yourself that need changing.

Time is very important. This is your life. Do not waste it.

Once you decide that you will only give one more chance to a person causing you pain, or not more than three months, you have saved yourself years and years of betrayal, anguish, and deterioration.

Your Friend.

CHAPTER 9: BUTTERFLIES

Who are we to judge how a person handles his emotional storm? Many have been destroyed or become crippled by it.

Some have walked similar paths ahead of us. They guide the way and inspire us. But a lot depends on what we have been through before and our inner strength, faith, and social support.

Those who have survived "well" have found themselves transformed with empathy, compassion, peace, the capacity to laugh again, and appreciation of the priorities in life.

They have gone through the pupa stage and emerged as butterflies!

But the butterflies have to be willing to fly into the unknown. And they do not look back.

Sex is not an appetite.

Can any other appetite create a human being?

Can any appetite cause physical pain to another human being?

No other appetite can cause so much physical and emotional pain to a child so created!

CHAPTER 10: SEX AND EMOTIONAL PAIN

I want to make a deal with you. I will give you intense physical pleasure for one hour.

In return, you must promise me the following.

You will stop your education.

You will fall below the poverty line.

You will agree to have only interrupted sleep for the next three to four years.

You will lose your freedom to go wherever you want, and whenever you want, for the next twenty years.

You will cause immense pain, physical and emotional to another completely innocent human being.

And you may murder this being and spend the rest of your life in jail.

Do we have a deal? Do you agree to all this?

Did you say, "No?" But you are agreeing to this every time you have sex without marriage!

Sex without responsibility for one's life (and that of another innocent human being) leads to severe emotional pain for the woman and child.

Sex is not an appetite.

What other appetite creates a third person?
What other appetite causes so much emotional pain?

The American medical profession has twice relinquished its leadership and jumped on the public bandwagon for the sake of popularity.

This is one of the two. And the hospitals have jumped on the wagon, too! They send you magazines teaching you to have a healthy sexual appetite.

They have lost their minds. To say that sex is one of our natural appetites is the height of irresponsibility.

It permits you to jump into as many beds as you want and have as many pregnancies as you want. Then you have children that you will starve to death, throw them out of the car, or leave them in foster homes because you never thought about the time and responsibilities of children when you were enjoying sex.

And then you will go to jail for child abuse, child neglect, and infanticide.

Your life is destroyed. You have given your children extreme emotional pain, and you now have extreme emotional pain.

Be very clear. Sex means that a man puts the seed of his future children in you. That is it.

If you put a plant in the soil, it will take root. Your child will be born whether you want it or not.

What appetite for eating and drinking puts a seed of a child in you?

The American Medical Association has lost its qualifications to think!

Men will call sex "an appetite," "making love," "sexual freedom," or anything else as long as they can "brainwash" a woman into giving them the freedom to indulge in it.

They want it so bad that if the woman refuses, they are capable of raping her. For them, it is an hour of fun with no strings attached.

Guess who has to pay the price?

Think about this. You can eat and drink as much as you want, yet you cannot create another human being! You cannot create President Biden or Hitler. But eating and drinking are considered appetites in the same category as sex!

If you put a seed into the soil, a plant will sprout. This needs a "force" pushing the seed to change into a plant with a stem, roots, leaves, and fruits.

With sex, the man forces his seed into you and creates the arms, legs, eyes, brain, and heart of a being that can bring terror to this world.

Which other appetite does that?

Sex is power, a force given to us, and like any force, it can create or destroy. Therefore, it has to be handled responsibly.

Do we not handle electricity with responsibility? It can give us immense benefits, but it can also electrocute us.

What other appetite causes so much emotional pain to the most helpless of our population?

Look at the foster-care children who have no bonding with any human being and the children given up for adoption. Then we act surprised when these neglected children attack and destroy us.

Can any other appetite give lifelong pain?

Your children have lifelong pain because you wanted a moment of fun!

What appetite leads to the murders of others?

Look at all the infanticides and abortions.

What appetite can lead a girl to drop out of school and become poor?

Sex is not an appetite. It is a tremendous creative force.

It is an act of procreation to be entered only when you have the finances, willingness, and wisdom to fulfill the responsibilities of taking care of a new human being. And that too for years to come!

When we bring a dog home, we know we will be taking care of it for years. We will feed it, take it to the vet, and take it for a walk, and we will be ready to fulfill our responsibilities.

So why are we not ready to fulfill our responsibilities every time we have sex?

It is unfortunate but true that only a marriage license can force a man to do this. He will run away the next morning.

But a woman is now left with a child to raise for the next twenty years. She has lost her freedom. She has to stay awake at night, changing diapers and trying to soothe a crying child. She has to stop her education and suddenly has no time left for employment. So now she is poor as well.

There goes her freedom, money, time, energy, and fun. Is that not self-destructive for a woman?

Who told her that she could have the same freedom as a man **when her body is different and the consequences for her are different?**

It is, therefore, totally her responsibility to say, "No. This is not an appetite. I will not indulge in such an act until I find a partner who is willing to share his money, time, and responsibility to take care of my child so created.

And the more a woman values herself, the more she holds herself in high esteem, the more firm she will be, and astonishingly, the more a man will respect her for having self-control and intelligence.

During the "cavemen period," everyone had sex anytime with everyone else.

The terrible pain and chaos that followed made every society, in every part of the world, come up with the idea of marriage.

And now we are willing to throw away all that wisdom of five thousand years for half an hour of fun? Does that make us intelligent human beings?

The leaders of the film and entertainment industry must be severely punished for brainwashing our teenagers that it is okay to immediately jump into bed when one is physically attracted to someone. They are responsible for all the unwanted children and their suffering and death. They must be made to pour their money into the care and education of every such child created.

It is very important to know there is no equality in the "sex act." A man throws out, but a woman takes in. They do not both throw out. They do not both take in.

During sex, a man "throws out."

He throws out his seeds. Why would we feel responsible for what we throw out? We throw out the garbage all the time!

During sex, a woman takes in.

She takes in his seed. When we take in something, we become responsible for it. When we value ourselves and have self-respect, we are very careful about who or what we let in, whether in our house or our bodies.

Sex is not an appetite. It is a force given to create a child.

Tell your daughters not to have sex before marriage.

Do not let them be alone with boys without a chaperone.

Set a good example yourself.

PART 3: CHRONIC EMOTIONAL PAIN

"The environment that causes pain cannot allow healing."

Buddha.

CHAPTER 11: CHRONIC PAIN

In chronic pain, your recovery depends either upon your removal from your environment or the removal of the cause of the pain.

Chronic pain arises when you do not take care of yourself and your welfare.

You have to take oxygen first yourself to live to help others.

The pain will occur if you do not take charge of your life and do not make your own decisions about where and how you will live.

It will occur if you have an addiction called dependency.

It will occur if you have no self-value, self-worth, self-respect, self-confidence, or self-protection.

It will occur if you allow toxic people to stay in contact with you.

But it will also occur from circumstances completely beyond your control.

Chronic non-relenting pain occurs:

in abuse,

when staying with non-caring people,

or those who are irresponsible or undependable, rude and insulting,

immoral,

out to hurt you because of their power,

steal your wealth or power,

who are willing to betray your trust,

who use you for their financial gain,

who treat you as a slave,

or are unpredictable. They can suddenly change from laughing to being furious.

To stay with a person abusing you is *not* nobility or love.

It is a lack of self-respect and a fear of being alone.

But this enables him to continue his abusive behavior, which will get worse.

Only by removing him from your life will six things happen.

He learns that he cannot get away with abusive behavior.

He will learn self-control.

So, he will have to grow up!

You will prevent further pain to yourself.

You will restore your self-respect.

And you have prevented others from being hurt by him.

Nobility never means a person should not be punished for his wrong deeds.

He must be punished as a deterrent to prevent recurrence.

You need the following to handle the pain:

A. Go to the Part 5, "Handle the Pain." This includes the stages of "roll with the pain," "deal with the pain," "heal from the pain," and so on.

B. Also consider the following.

1. Understand that love must never be "unconditional."

Abusers have put forward this belief so that they do not have to change, just as they put forward the statement that "quality time is better than quantity time,' so that they can avoid their responsibilities. Why do you accept it? Even God has a condition that you must be good in order for Him to love you. See the chapter on "Unconditional love."

2. Acceptance

There are to be no false hopes. Refusing to accept that the situation is irreversible or hoping that things may change is the cause of deep emotional turmoil.

Accept that a relationship has ended through death, divorce, or otherwise. It may be with your child.

If a relationship continually causes pain, it must be put to an end.

You have to end it to prevent it from spreading like gangrene and destroying your life.

Accept that "they are who they are." Maybe they decided to reject you. Perhaps they were selfish, abusive, greedy, cruel, or unfaithful. They betrayed your trust.

Accept your shortcomings and now work on removing them. There may be a lack of interpersonal skills, self-value, or self-respect. You may have controlling behavior or selfishness.

Accept that it may not be your fault.

3. Purpose

Determine a purpose for existence.

Your purpose in existence cannot be another person or the way of life you were used to. This is easier said than done and is almost impossible if you have a dependency or consider yourself the extension of someone's personality.

Your purpose now is to survive without increasing the damage to yourself for one year. You are about to go through a tunnel of fire.

If you can hang on long enough, the person who comes out from the other end will be quite different and stronger.

Why should you do so? Life is not worth living. Well, your children may need money or need to be rescued from something. Your ex-spouse may remarry, go to jail, become ill, and even die, and now the children need to return to you.

Perhaps in the future, your children may face a calamity, and your example is what will give them the courage to go forward. Does not every animal prepare its young one for how to handle life?

4. Discipline

You will need daily self-discipline to handle the pain and grow strong.

Once you are calm and your life is peaceful, people may or may not come back. Perhaps you would not want them back. However, other people will walk into your life because of your new vibrations since you have learned to strengthen your core.

PART 4: MEDICATION

Stress is part of life. It was given to you to develop. It helps you to grow mentally and spiritually.

Do not ask for medication for stress.

Deal with it by your character.

CHAPTER 12: MEDICATIONS

Why do you take psychiatric medicine? Is it because you cannot handle anxiety or stress? But these are emotions. Emotions should not be handled by medication.

And, by facing these emotions, you would truly grow up.

Did not the pioneers cross the prairies and go into unknown face stress? They had no medication. But they had the maturity to understand that one deals with whatever life throws at you without medication.

Note the following:

The minute you stop the medicine, the pain comes back.

Why did it come back? Why did the medicine not eradicate the pain?

This means you will need the medicine for the rest of your life. Worse still, you will progress from one medicine to two, then to three, and more. Is that what you really want?

This is because these medicines can only **block** emotions. They **cannot remove** the emotions of pain, despair, terror, anguish, rage, jealousy, and so on. The minute the medicine is stopped, the emotion announces its existence.

Since an emotion gets stronger every day **because you focus on it,** the drug stops being effective, and another medication must be added.

Psychiatric medications are needed when a person is in such a fog that he cannot think straight (as observed by mental specialists) or has not learned self-control or self-discipline. The fog can be delusion or paranoia. The medication is to be given for a limited time (not more than a few months) and must be accompanied by counseling. The counseling has to focus on personal development with a change in attitude and outlook on life.

Medication is also given when a person is damaged by an illness and can no longer function normally and take care of himself or his outbursts. Examples are mental retardation and Huntington's chorea.

To take medication because you have an "attention deficit disorder, or stress," will only damage you. These can be handled by learning self-control, self-discipline, and self-development.

A word of caution here. These medicines cannot be stopped suddenly. They must be tapered under the guidance of a physician.

We have become zombies, dependent on drugs. We want to take medication to not be distracted, for ADD, to not be depressed, to not be anxious, to sleep, or to be awake. We have become dolls with no willpower over our lives.

And, as the drugs lose their effectiveness, we progress from one drug to seven drugs, continuing to ruin our lives.

Any medication that is taken for our minds affects our lives profoundly. It affects our ability to make clear decisions or to work well. We are in great anxiety if we do not get our "fix" because we have become addicted to our medication.   An addict is always weak. He lacks internal strength. He can be manipulated.

We are controlled by our feelings instead of controlling them.

What happened to willpower and courage?

Why have we given up on our character?

And we teach our children that they cannot handle life without medication.

We can finally grow up and acquire peace only when we trust our character instead of a pill.

Stress is part of life. It is not a reason for medication.

PART 5: HANDLE THE PAIN

CHAPTER 13: TIME INVOLVED IN HEALING

This is from the start of the pain. Though sorrow is a part of you, it will keep decreasing in intensity. That is why it is said that "time is a great healer."

But we are talking about how long it takes for you to return to your routine and work as before.

This is never a fixed number and can be less or more. It depends upon your inner makeup, beliefs, culture, how you have seen others handle it, how the movies have shown you to handle it (and they are always wrong), what else you have gone through in life, and if you are on medication.

So one sees Mrs. Kennedy stoically standing as her husband's bier passes by. We may see another person shouting, screaming, and thrashing because she never learned to control her emotions.

If a person recovers in a few weeks, it does not mean that he grieves less. He may need the money to survive. He may want to grieve privately. He may need to appear natural for the sake of his children or his aging parents.

But an estimate should be given.

It took nine months to create you.

It should take nine to twelve months to become a stable new person.

This does not mean that you do not have to go back to work. Depending upon the relationship, one should return to work after two weeks to two months. Work helps. It also does not mean that we should not start enjoying our lives again earlier.

CHAPTER 14: HOW TO HANDLE PAIN

Value Time

One must not underestimate time. Time is the great healer. It helps our emotions ebb away. Things will be handled better after some time. When we are in the acute onslaught of pain, we cannot think clearly, but the emotions ebb, and acceptance comes later.

Time also helps us recover once we fix a goal ("I will try this for nine to twelve months)."

Time starts helping us from the moment we focus on one day at a time. Just getting through that day puts less burden upon us than trying to recover completely.

The Steps

A. The "Pause."

B. Roll with the pain

C. Deal with the pain

D. Heal from the pain

E. Rebuild

Each stage has a different time period and it is always a range rather than an arbitrary figure.

Each stage will also vary in intensity with different individuals.

Each step follows the same format:

1. Pause: No immediate decision. No immediate action.

2. The Time Set.

3. No Medication

4. No Complications.

5. Cry

6. Routine

7. Work hard

8. Rest

9. Family (take care of your family responsibilities)

10. Socially

11. Nature walks without any listening device, iPhone, or music.

12. Analyze.

In the second and third stages, we add the following.

Goal.
Acceptance.
Affirmation: I did not ask for this sort of life, but I received it and must live it in the best possible way.

CHAPTER 15: THE "SEVEN-STEP" PROGRAM

Two things are important.

First, be careful who you associate with. The objective is not only to heal but to prevent a recurrence.

Second, you have to make your core strong. For this, the program of seven steps is outlined below.

1. Be careful who you associate with.

In our lives, we may come upon a person who may lead us to addiction, land us in jail, take away our children and turn our loved ones against us, cause us to lose our wealth, or lead us to suicide or murder! No matter how nice, charming, and fun he is, he will cause us immense suffering. Such a person can destroy us!

Second, if we stay with a person, we will eventually become like him. If you put an object next to a radioactive material, it will absorb its nature. If you stay with angry, non-caring, irresponsible, immoral, abusive, or evil people, you will eventually become this person.

That is the basis of the saying, "Tell me who your friends are, and I will tell you who you are." Be very careful of the company you keep! Do not be over-friendly, but study the person. The best time to know who he is like is when his needs clash with yours or when he is angry or frustrated.

The Seven-Step Program. Set a time for one year.

1. Pause (This has already been described and is critical).

2. Roll With the Pain

3. Deal with the pain.

4. Heal from the pain.

5. Continue Healing

6. Rebuild.

7. Then live the "Critical One Year." It helps to do this with someone who can give you support.

Learn why it is important "to pretend an emotion."

Do not go by what people promise for the future, but by what they did in the past. Do you have the willpower to do this, especially when they are pleading for reconciliation? It is ultimately your decision.

Forgiveness never means allowing people back into your life to hurt you again. Instead, forgiveness means you do not burn over what they did and wish them no ill will.

You have to make your core strong. This can only be done by self-control, self-discipline, character, moral beliefs, and faith. And you need energy. There is a chapter on energy ahead.

An important advancement is made when a man begins to lean on himself for support, instead of others or medication. He is learning to draw his courage out.

His Mantra should be, "I will handle today, not in emotional turmoil but with acceptance. I will heal and rebuild even though I do not want to, but I must give myself one year. This much I owe to myself!"

CHAPTER 16: ROLL WITH THE PAIN

(Pause/ Roll/ Deal/ Heal/ Rebuild)

Pause: No Immediate Decision and No Immediate Action.

Do not kill another. Do not kill yourself. The one thing that can save you from ruining your life is that your reaction must have no revenge.

The time involved:

One to a few weeks

Do not take medication.

No complications:

Do not jump into bed with anyone. Do not give up your job, donate your property or money, or sign blank papers.

Cry:

You are crying constantly or off and on, or you may be frozen in grief. Your pain completely takes control of you. The body creates only so much energy per day and you are using every bit of it to go through the pain.

Routine

Unable to have a routine

Work hard

Unable to work

Rest

Resting in fits and starts or when exhausted.

Family:

You cannot take care of others. They have to take care of you.

Socially

You do not wish to speak to anyone.

Nature Walks without any listening device, phone, music, or lectures.

You are not able to.

Analyze.

You are devastated. Your thoughts include the following: "How could this happen?

How could he/she /they do this to me?

What do I do now?

How can I live now?

I do not even want to live!

Where do I go from here?"

CHAPTER 17: DEAL WITH THE PAIN

(Pause/ Roll/ Deal/ Heal/ Rebuild)

Pause: No Immediate Decision and No Immediate Action.

Do not kill another. Do not kill yourself.

The one thing that can save you from ruining your life is that your reaction must have no revenge.

The time involved:

A few weeks to a few months.

No medication.

No complications:

Emotionally: Do not jump into bed with anyone. Do not have affairs.

Financially: Do not donate your property or money. Do not sign blank papers. Do not resign. Find someone to run your business while you recover. And later go back. Your job offers human contact, distractions, and self-respect.

You need the job more than the job needs you!

Cry:

You will be crying off and on.

Routine:

Have a routine from the time you wake up to the time you sleep. This is important.

Work hard:

Clean your house, scrub the floor, Cook, Paint the walls.

Physical Rest:

Have a routine for resting during the day and at night. Even if you do not sleep at night, wake up at the same time to develop your self-discipline. You can catch up on your sleep during the day.

Mental Rest:

As Rudolf Steiner said, the brain, like your muscles, needs rest to carry its load. If your arm gets tired from carrying a load, you rest it a while, and it can carry the load again.

Similarly, your brain is carrying a tremendous load of grief, despair, and anger. You need to rest it daily so that it can carry its load again. How do you do that? See the chapter called "Continue healing."

Family:

Take care of your family, dependents, parents, children, spouse, pets, etc. It helps you heal and gives you self-worth. Talk to your family.

Socially:

Social support is important. Start by talking to total strangers casually. Do not tell them about your personal life.

Nature Walks without any listening device, phone, music, or lectures:

You must face yourself and your loneliness in this walk **without** any distractions from your iPhone, music, or lectures. Handle the silence. Handle the loneliness. Go through your sorrow. Think ahead. This allows your inner strength to start to emerge.

Analyze.

You are devastated. Your thoughts include the following:

How could this happen?

How could he/she /they do this to me?

What do I do now?

How can I live now?

I do not want to live!

Where do I go from here?

"You have to let go of the thing breaking you even if it breaks you to let it go!" (Author unknown).

A shorter program is presented to deal with the pain. It is called The S.T.O.P. Program.

CHAPTER 18: THE "S.T.O.P." PROGRAM

S.T.O.P. is the acronym for handling pain or depression.

S is for "Substitute." Substitute your emotion of sorrow/depression with cheerfulness. Pretend an emotion. See below.

T is for "Time." Fix a time of thirty days.

O is for "Organization." Organize your whole day.

P is for "Purpose." Right now, your purpose is to get through the thirty days.

The S.T.O.P. program initially lasts for thirty days but involves *active participation.* Therefore, you need to do your homework.

Your Homework:

1. Mix with people

Pain or depression intensifies in solitude. It is very important to mingle with people, talk to them, and exchange ideas. People get uplifted by each other. Their moods shift by the people they meet. Sometimes, you might hear something that is mind-changing.

2. "Walk and talk."

Go for a walk and greet or talk to the people you meet. Also, go to community centers and senior centers. But people will not talk to you if you have a grumpy face,

3. Exercise.

Energy Begets Energy. Force yourself to exercise, if only for thirty minutes a day.

4. Your Attitude and gratitude.

You will overcome your sadness if you have gratitude, curiosity, and purpose,

5. Acquire knowledge.

Knowledge is power! Read the Part on "Emotions," and the one entitled "Get Strong."

After the thirty-day course finishes, you can repeat this one more time or go to the one-year course outlined in the chapter called "The Critical Year."

Depression is to be attacked by *pretending* to be enthusiastic, grateful, curious, and willing to learn and advance your intelligence.

What is one year? Would you not prefer to enter the afterlife with more intelligence than you currently possess?

Why pretend? This is described in the chapter on "Emotions." If you "pretend" long enough, you can develop the emotion.

Remember that the one reason you came on this earth is to develop.

And the current situation is given to you to develop, provided you ask,

"What can I learn from this?"

Without acceptance, and

without letting go of your past life,

you cannot move forward.

You can stay in a corner crying for the rest of your life.

Or, you can say, "This is what life has thrown at me. But there is a purpose why I am still alive. I must conquer my emotions and live to the best of my ability to achieve this purpose."

CHAPTER 19: HEAL FROM THE PAIN

(Pause/ Roll/ Deal/ Heal/ Rebuild)

Pause: *Do not kill another. Do not kill yourself.*

The one thing that can save you from ruining your life is that your reaction must have no revenge.

The time involved:

It is from the third month to some months.

No medication.

No complications:

Emotionally: Do not jump into bed with anyone. Do not have affairs.

Financially: Do not donate your property or money. Do not sign blank papers. Do not resign. Find someone to run your business while you recover. And go back. Your job offers human contact, distractions, and self-respect.

You need the job more than the job needs you!

Cry:

You will be crying off and on.

But now, you should have a fixed time in the day or evening when you do not think about your pain.

You are doing this to rest your brain and to get self-discipline, which will bring you willpower.

Routine:

Have a routine from the time you wake up to the time you sleep.

Work hard:

Get back to your old routine. But do hard physical work one day a week.

Physical Rest:

Have a routine for resting during the day and at night. Even if you do not sleep at night, wake up at the same time to develop your self-discipline. You can catch your sleep during the day.

Mental Rest:

As Rudolf Steiner said, the brain, like your muscle, needs rest to carry its load. If your arm gets tired from carrying a load, you rest it a while, and it can carry the load again.

Similarly, your brain is carrying a tremendous load of grief, despair, and anger. You need to rest it daily so that it can carry its load again.

How do you do that?

Read the next chapter, "Continue to heal."

Family:

Take care of your family, dependents, parents, children, spouse, pets, etc. It helps you heal and gives you self-worth. Talk to your family.

Socially:

Social support is important. You may or may not be all alone. Develop a social support system. As you meet the same strangers every day, friendships will form. Some people will leave you. They were meant to leave you.

Nature Walks without any listening device, iPhone, music, or lectures:

You must face yourself and your loneliness in this walk *without any distractions*. Face the pain. Go through your sorrow. Think ahead.

No addict can achieve this, and if you cannot even take a walk without a phone or music, you are addicted. Then, you crave anti-anxiety and anti-depressant medication. Why are you so anxious to see what everyone is saying when it is so important to face your thoughts alone?

You have never allowed yourself to face the quiet loneliness and let the Cosmos fill your inner emptiness with comfort and strength. When we are alone without iPhones or music and face life alone, inner strength comes, as do insights and wisdom.

Why do you think Buddha stayed alone for six years or Christ went into the wilderness?

When we are alone without any distractions, we remove our outer layer, let the Universe soothe and comfort us, and give us the thoughts we need to recover. It does not happen overnight. You cannot shed your outer layer in a day.

Analyze.

Accept that what happened was either because of the decisions you made or decisions someone else made, or they were acts of nature.

So, the first step is **acceptance**. Accept your destiny.

The second step is to **protect yourself**. After a few weeks, you must **stop** yourself from crying about it constantly. This is how you protect yourself from your emotions.

The third step is to **stop** feeling sorry for yourself.

The fourth step is to **stop** hoping the past will come back.

The fifth step is to **start carrying** out your responsibilities instead of depending on others, even if you have physical limitations. You are going to live despite your limitations.

The sixth step is to **go to** homeless shelters or soup kitchens and help someone physically daily.

Love this small child inside you. Stop her hurting and teach her to stand on her feet.

CHAPTER 20: CONTINUE TO HEAL

Give your brain a break!

1. Acceptance

Accept that what has happened has happened. Things will not go back to what they were, *no matter how desperately you want this.*

This acceptance takes a long time to arrive at. You also have to accept the rejection, failure, infidelity, or abuse that has happened to you. This finality is a painful reality! But acceptance sets you free to progress.

2. Take care of yourself.

Nourish Yourself. You took care of others, and they did not suffer. You did not take care of yourself, so you suffered. Now is the time for you to nourish yourself in terms of rest, food, and exercise. Take care of your welfare.

3. Be kind to yourself.

Forgive yourself. As long as you did the best you could, with the knowledge you had then and in the circumstances that existed, that is all that counts.

4. Give your brain a break.

Your brain has been under severe strain. Give rest to your brain daily by distracting yourself. Talk to people about other topics. Go for a walk. Watch a movie.

5. Stay away from psychiatric medications.

For the mind to make the correct decisions, it must be free from medication, and it must be free from emotions. This requires personal growth. Unless you are falling apart and need medication for a short time (a few months), stay away from psychiatric medications. Go through this fire of pain, and you will emerge stronger at the other end.

6. **Have the same fixed time daily when you try not to think about the pain.**

How do you do this?

Distract yourself at times with a book, show, movie, pets, or talk to someone.

Displace your thought with another at such times: "I will not think about this right now."

Read the chapter "Why Pretend?" in the next part.

8. Decisions. I must try this for a year.

I cannot control the actions of others. I can only control my reaction. My reaction must not include revenge.

Leave the one who did not care that his action caused you pain. It is easier said, but if you have self-respect, it will help.

9. Can you get away from the place of pain?

This is valid only in situations of abuse.

10. Do not be afraid to be alone. Do not fear change.

There is no harm in trying this for a year.

11. Pets.

There is nothing like pets to heal us. Have them in twos. As you see them interact with each other, you forget your troubles for some time.

Second, taking care of pets brings a routine that is soothing to the hurt soul. You have a fixed time to wake up, feed them, take them for a walk, and play with them.

Third, their unconditional love when they greet you heals you, as do their antics.

12. A word about routine.

Routine is soothing. Any prisoner can tell you how much anxiety is produced when the routine is lost. There is a routine of daily activities: waking and sleeping at a fixed time, getting ready, taking care of pets, doing your work, and the evening routine. What is not soothing is the jarring effect of changing this as per your whims.

13. Let us pretend to be cheerful.

Pretend for a month and see what happens.

14. Develop your spirituality

Learn to pray. Prayer gives you strength, courage, and wisdom. But your prayer should be reverent. Pray, "Give me the courage and strength to handle what I am going through. Guide me."

Always keep silent for a while after you speak so that His Grace and Wisdom can come to you. How can you hear if you keep talking? Your present situation is unbearable. Prayer helps. Pray for inner strength.

15. Seek Guidance.

Seek guidance from people, online sources, self-help books, and your Creator.

CHAPTER 21: ENERGY BEGETS ENERGY

Emotional pain depletes our energy. So does depression and fear. So does the aftermath of anger.

When we sit around and do not move, the water from our blood seeps into our muscles and makes them heavy. The heavy muscles then press on our nerves and cause pain. The heavy muscles pull on our bones and cause pain. Since we are not moving, calcium leeks from our bones and muscles, weakening them. Our heart gets weaker.

This is why exercise is so important. Even if we wish to die, let us have energy until the end!

Energy Is Electricity.

If a dynamo does not move, no electricity is produced. We are a bundle of electricity. Our electrical impulses can be medically picked up. We get our energy from air, water, food, and light, but to convert this energy into "functional power," we must move.

Has anyone seen energy? No. Similar to the case of God, we can only see the "effects" of energy.

Finite Energy

Despite all our resources, we can only produce a limited amount of energy per day.

When we get a wound or an illness, energy is used up in the recovery process.

Energy is used in healing after other people's actions or words hurt us.

Energy is used up in handling our emotional pain.

Energy is used up in trying to understand why we are abused.

Energy is used up by the abused in taking care of the abusers and those who reject him or treat him with anger and contempt. So he has nothing left to calm and heal himself, recover from illness, get his inner strength, or plan his future. This is why it is self-destructive to take care of abusers.

To Heal, We Need Our Energy.

We preserve the energy we have by staying away from toxic people

And we create energy by moving and exercising.

CHAPTER 22: CARE FOR YOURSELF

Take care of yourself as you would for another person or your child. First, take oxygen to yourself before you give it to another, or you will pass out.

Care for yourself enough to leave an abusive environment immediately.

Care for yourself enough to see that you are safe and have some means of sustenance.

Sacrifice does not mean ignoring your physical, emotional, financial, and social well-being.

To recover from emotional pain, you need clarity of mind. For clarity of mind, you need to get rid of any addictions, including dependency, medications, and chemicals.

Care for yourself enough to get free from emotional pain. Sometimes, this can only come by letting go of those who do not want to come to you. You can protect them from afar. Your first duty is your survival.

Care about yourself enough to accept what you cannot have now. You still have this life to live.

The mind can only take so much from the constant toxic effects of emotional pain. Care for yourself enough to set aside time daily when the mind can relax and rejuvenate.

You cannot get well in isolation. You need social support, but take care not to complicate your life with affairs while recovering from emotional pain.

CHAPTER 23: REBUILD

(Pause/ Roll/ Deal/ Heal/ Rebuild)

This is your year of growth. But, as long as you sit around passively and helpless, feeling sorry for yourself and waiting for others to improve your life, you will not heal. Other people will not make your life better. Why should they? It is a waste of time and energy for them! It is your life. You must make it better yourself.

This is not to be a passive time where you lie around depressed. You have to change yourself. This involves a lot of work.

You are like the caterpillar that has to turn into a butterfly.

From the stages of anger, shock, anguish, despair, and pain, you have to progress to be a pain-free individual with self-confidence, curiosity, and peace. Is that not worth the pain?

But you have to go through this "pupa stage" to do this. It is a long and painful tunnel, but what awaits you at the other end is worth it. What a journey! Are you afraid to try it?

You have a lot of work to do now.

It is now over three to six months. You are entering a time of "personal growth." You have to finish picking up all the pieces you were shattered into and put them together to become whole again.

1. Start with a time limit.

Your goal is one year, after which you will review your progress and what you have learned.

2. Increase your inner strength

The daily practice of self-control and self-discipline are the keys to becoming strong. So is willpower. The more you deny yourself. The stronger you get. So, do not eat the cake you want. Do not look at your iPhone for one hour in the morning and while walking or driving.

3. Stop feeling sorry for yourself

To feel sorry for yourself after three months becomes selfish because all you are thinking about is, "Poor me!" What are you achieving? It makes you passive and removes any incentive to take action to improve your life."

You are turned inwards. You have to turn outwards.

Feeling sorry for yourself removes the zest for life and prevents curiosity and hope from moving in.

4. Take charge of your life

"Growing up "means that you make your own decisions for your work, happiness, and welfare. Do not blindly do what others want you to so that you may be considered "nice." A child does that.

5. Rely on yourself to get what you want

Do not wait for others to do so. Years will go by before they will move. Do not worry that you may make mistakes. Everyone does. Have the strength to correct them.

6. Do not be blind in your trust.

Do not give away your power. Instead, keep your money and social support.

7. Protect your dignity

Protect your dignity, that of your family, your status, and the dignity of your profession. Do not invite contempt by your actions.

Every scenario that life throws at you offers you a choice to either develop or succumb to bitterness, despair, and so deteriorate.

At least show your Guides that you did your best to develop before you left the earth.

CHAPTER 24: HOW TO REBUILD

To rebuild is a challenging task. You have to rise from your ashes, start again, and rebuild your life, even when you do not want to.

How do you rebuild your life?

Leaving is critical.

To rebuild, you have to remove everyone who caused you pain. This way, you have the energy to heal and rebuild. Even if the people who hurt you apologize and wish to make amends, you must stay away for **one or two years** to grow up. Only then can you get clarity on what happened and the motives behind it, as well as get new perspectives. This requires willpower.

If you remain in contact with them, they may inadvertently remind you of how they hurt you or cause you fresh pain, and now you need energy to heal from this and have less for rebuilding.

It is only then that you will find that people acted selfishly. They discovered that you had no self-value, self-worth, or self-confidence, so they took advantage of you. They saw that you did not have self-protection and so could betray your trust. They saw that you could not emotionally leave them and had no other support, and so they could abuse you.

As you emerge from your emotional pain, you will get this clarity. If you stay with them, they will steal your life force and leave you an empty shell.

But if you must stay in contact with them because of children, work, or legal matters, keep your conversation to the minimum and through a third person.

Acceptance is critical.

Accept the finality of the situation, however painful that may be. This is the most difficult part.

Timing is critical.

Have a goal of one year. And start one day at a time.

Social interaction is critical.

Meeting other people gives you distraction, comfort, healing, and different perspectives. It may also open other avenues of life. You may have lost everyone in your life. But friends and work will fill the hole and help in healing.

What do you rebuild?

Build Physically

Value your appearance. Dress well.
Value the appearance of your home and surroundings.

Build your Home Atmosphere.

Get rid of anyone who pollutes your atmosphere with anger, contempt, inconsideration, or rudeness and who does not share in the household chores and expenses. True love always has conditions. See the chapter on unconditional love.

Build Financially

Support yourself and be financially independent for now and in the future. It gives you self-worth. Live within your means.

Build Social Support

Rebuild your social acquaintances and slowly develop friendships. Go to places holding social activities.

Build your 'Boundaries."

These are your "moral boundary" and your "emotional boundary." Your emotional boundary keeps toxic people out.

Build your "Fifteen Selves." See the chapter ahead.

Build your "Nine Healths." These are given in no particular order:

Physical Health

Environmental Health

Work Health

Financial Health

Mental Health

Emotional Health

Moral Health

Social Health and

Spiritual Health

Fill in the gaps in your personal development. These are listed below.

What do you want to do, become bitter or better?

1. **Remove all addictions**
These include anger, greed, dependency, controlling behavior, as well as chemicals and drugs.

2. **Remove violence.**

3. **Develop humility and patience.** You cannot learn without them.

4. **Set your mental thermostat.**
Learn to set your mental "thermostat up to calmness or cheerfulness every morning.

5. **Do not blame your past for your present.**

Your personality is plastic and is always capable of great change. So is your mind. Blaming your past is trying to find a way to escape your responsibilities and accountabilities.

No court should accept this excuse!

What helps in rebuilding?

1. A purpose in life:

This may be just getting through the coming year. It may be taking care of those dependent on you. It may be to leave an example for your children. It may be to show God that you did your best.

2. Learn to master yourself.

Develop self-control by practicing respect, good manners, modesty, decency, and fairness at home.

Do what you should and *not what you want.* This is how you control yourself.

3. Live your life with balance.

Everything should be in moderation.

4. Share the chores of where you live.

5. Fulfill your responsibilities to each member of the family.

7. Have gratitude for what you do have.

8. Do charity.

As you rebuild, you start becoming happy and relaxed. Your cheerfulness, hopefulness, caring, and compassion will begin to emerge, attracting other people.

There can be no emotional health or mental health without moral health.

Moral health lays down the fabric of our character, the groundwork of rules and guideposts by which we are to live our lives. Lack of this is responsible for the pain in our lives and our society.

Moral health is completely separate from religion. Yet, it is adopted by every religion because it is so critical to our development. All these "Healths" are described in the author's book on personal development.

CHAPTER 25: THE CRITICAL YEAR

Before you kill yourself, you should live for one year at your highest level, offer excellence, and be happy!

How can you do this when you are suicidal? It will require a lot of determination. The present has unbearable pain, and the future is bleak. But we are talking about *one year* of your life. What have you got to lose? You will have the ability to say to your reception committee (after death) that you tried.

Let us seek some answers.

A. Be Happy.

How can you be happy when you are in so much pain? Read the chapter on "Pretend" in the part on Emotions.

B. What does 'offering excellence" mean?

Offering excellence means you could not do better than this. Offer excellence in your work.

C. What does the "highest level" mean?

It means controlling your emotions and not allowing them to control you.

And when we speak, we must do so with good manners because good manners are a sign of self-control, and self-control is one of the signs of inner strength!

Living at your highest level also means the following.

It is to accept rejection from your loved ones and others, however painful, *without feeling inferior.*

It is to be accountable for your actions instead of blaming them on others.

It is not to be in denial over anything.

It is to love and value yourself, your self-respect, and your welfare and happiness without being selfish.

Do not make impulsive decisions but consider the consequences of your actions.

It is to protect your mind by meditation, not medication.

It means to be focused, not distracted.

It is to be able to face fear without medication.

It is to be the same in good times and bad.

This year, you must also learn not to shout when you are speaking and not to repeat yourself more than twice.

When you open your mouth to speak, you must be modest, decent, and well-mannered. Your shouting, being rude, and insulting do not show that you are powerful. They show that you have no intelligence! Do not cause emotional pain by criticizing the place you visit.

To continue to keep speaking means that first, we are scared to let the other person speak because we know that he is right, and second, we are scared to think, and as long as we keep speaking, we do not have to think.

To keep repeating yourself or to speak needlessly is a sign of stupidity.

PART 6: EMOTIONS/ FEELINGS

We are also emotional beings. We will stumble through life unless we learn how to control our emotions.

We have no other way of controlling them except by always acting only according to moral principles.

Your emotions cover you like a blanket not allowing reasoning and self-protection to come through.

Control your emotions or they will control you!

Feelings are always fleeting. Only ethics/principles remain permanent.

When a man says that his feelings toward you have changed so he can leave you for another whenever he feels like it, it shows that he has no backbone. He has no moral principles and no responsibility toward maintaining the stability of a home for his children. He should be sent to jail for this.

This is why the institution of marriage was created: so that he could be punished for behaving so badly.

No therapy or medication can treat the Emotional Pain and Attention Deficiency Disorder caused by a lack of self-discipline.

CHAPTER 26: WHY PRETEND?

It sounds crazy to ask you to be happy when you are in so much pain. But we are talking about protecting your mind, which has been under unbelievable pressure!

If you are happy

When you are happy and feel gratitude for what you have, the hormones associated with happiness are released inside you, such as Serotonin, Dopamine, and Endorphins.

But, this cannot happen as long as your basic fulfilments are not met, such as food, shelter, freedom, and the absence of poverty.

Look around to see how you can be happy. Fix the same time every day when you will not think about your pain. Play with animals. Talk to people. Play a sport. Watch a funny movie. Read a funny book.

You also become happy when you are no longer brooding, feeling sorry for yourself, or being angry.

If you pretend to be happy

When you *pretend* to be happy daily, the same thing happens. The body produces these "happy hormones" according to what you "allegedly" feel.

Your body cannot tell whether you are really happy or merely "pretending to be happy."

Then, these hormones, in turn, start creating happiness inside you because they are "the happy hormones." This happiness is not contingent on anything outside. Nobody has to give you anything, and nothing has to happen to make you happy. True happiness comes from inside, not because you have a job, money, marriage, position, or wealth.

If you consistently "act happy," you become happy.

Repetition

Any emotion can become strong when you repeatedly focus on it.

So can depression.

If you act calm for a year, you will become calm.

If you act angry repeatedly, you will become an angry person.

If you are fearful repeatedly, you will stay fearful.

If you think of your hatred for someone repeatedly, your hatred will grow.

If you repeatedly say that life is not worth living, you will start acting on it.

On the other hand, if you repeatedly think of life with gratitude and reverence, you will start believing in it.

Try it for a year.!

CHAPTER 27: DO YOU LIVE BY YOUR FEELINGS?

Then feelings are your masters! Feelings are also called emotions. You cannot have peace or true happiness because you are like a puppet that is always being pulled in different directions by his feelings. You have to resort to lies, and you will ruin your life and your career.

When a man has no morals to guide him, he will act according to his feelings. He can only be controlled by laws or fear because he does not know how to control himself.

This has disastrous results, which are painful to everyone affected. When such a man is angry, he will be insulting and violent. When he is selfish, he will be unfair. When he faces a bad time, he will kill himself. **He has no self-control. He does whatever his emotions tell him to do**. Since his emotions remove his thinking power, he lands in jail or has a divorce. The movies encourage this by showing a man destroying things when he is angry. (The movie industry should be punished for setting bad examples).

However, a man with self-control and self-discipline will put his feelings aside and act according to his principles and ethics. He has a moral map that tells him how to behave. *Where is your moral map?* He has advanced in his personal development. The front part of his brain can now control the headquarters of his emotions, which are located in the central part of his brain!

He acts as he should, not as he wants.

This is why *self-control* is one of the first things we must teach our children. Coupled with *handling frustration without violence* and *delaying gratification*, they will learn self-mastery.

But this can only be done by setting an example yourself! You, as an adult, must be able to show good manners at home. You should keep your voice low and your hands by your side when angry. But how can you have self-mastery when you are already an addict? You are addicted to your iPhone.

Control of your addiction is the first step in self-mastery.

Control of your speech is the second step in self-mastery. You show self-mastery when you do not shout, curse, or are vulgar in your language.

Think of emotions as separate living beings inside your head whose only goal is to control you and become your masters.

So, you blindly listen and act when they tell you to lie and cheat, skip your class, not do your homework, or jump into bed with someone without thinking of the consequences. When they tell you to hurt someone, you hurt, and if they direct you to rape or kill, you rape and kill.

But you have often seen yourself separate from them. At times, you refused to listen to them. When your emotions told you to go out and play, you said, "No, I need to finish my homework first." When they told you to eat that cake, you refused.

Your mind can overcome your emotions.

It is critical to know that your mind is separate from your emotions. It is important to know that your emotions are always struggling to be in control of your mind.

But to do this, emotions have to make your mind weak. You become weaker whenever you give in to your feelings or act impulsively.

CHAPTER 28: THE RULES OF EMOTIONS/FEELINGS

All emotions follow the same rules:

1. **Conquer an emotion, or it will conquer you.** An emotion wants to overcome and master you.

By giving in to your feelings, emotions become stronger.

It is important to know that emotions are like little people inside you. They are always struggling to get power over you. They always want to control your mind. They can then direct you to destroy your or another's life. But to do this, emotions have to make your mind weak. This is described in the book on personal development.

There are two types of emotions in us: the good and the bad. The bad ones want to control you. They want you to be depressed or angry. They want you to hurt others with your tongue and actions. They may even want you to commit suicide! They don't care that when you die, they die as well. The thrill of being in power for a time has been worth it to them.

2. **Emotion is most intense initially.**

That is when it will block all reasoning. So, do not make decisions on the spot. Instead, give yourself a week or month unless it is in defense of someone, yourself, or your country.

3. **Do not make impulsive decisions.**

An impulsive decision is one made on your feelings.

4. **Do not go extreme in your emotions.**

If you do not go overboard in joy, you will not go overboard in sorrow.

5. The more you focus on emotion, the larger and more intense it becomes. An example is starting by being angry and then going blind with rage. Or you focus on your fear, leading to a panic attack!

6. And the more you fight against a particular emotion, the stronger it gets because you focus on it so much. Distraction is the key.

7. The less you focus on it, the faster it shrinks. This is done by distraction, displacement, dilution with other thoughts, and willpower. An emotion always gets weaker when you do not focus on it. Focus on something else. The key to overcoming an emotion is by refusing to think about it. This is done by distraction. Read a book, Talk with some people. Watch a movie.

8. An emotion can be overcome by substituting it with another.

If you force yourself to become calm when you are furious, you become calm.

9. You cannot hold two opposite emotions at the same time. You cannot have love and hatred for the same person at the same time. You cannot have depression and gratitude at the same moment.

This is a vital point. Because if you are depressed but replace it with thoughts of gratitude and cheerfulness, you can conquer depression. Read the chapter on "Pretend".

10. To control you, an emotion must remove your capacity to think! This is why you later regret what you did. You cannot understand how you went blind with rage and killed someone. Why did your fear make you push away another person and take his seat in the lifeboat?

On the other hand, other people have faced their fears and still acted the right way because they have learned to be in charge of their emotions.

11. Bad emotions prevent you from protecting yourself. They prevent clarity of mind. They can make you lose interest in work, life, or love. You become depressed. They can make you take the life of another or your own!

12. If you pretend to have an emotion, you will start developing it. If you pretend to be calm daily for a month, you will become calm. When you act grateful daily, you will become grateful.

If you pretend to be cheerful and upbeat daily for a month, you will start becoming cheerful.

13. Antidepressants and anti-anxiety medications stop you from developing power over your emotions.

14. An emotion cannot win if you are stronger.

You get stronger by practicing willpower, self-control, and self-discipline.

15. Your greatest strength is to live by Moral Rules /Ethics. Then you know what you should or should not do!

If you have to ask every time whether "there is a law against what I am doing?" then you have completely closed your conscience and moral sense. You have been reduced to living only by the laws of your country.

Remember there was no law against having slaves at one time. Did that make it right?

Laws did not allow women to vote. Was that right?

There was no law against children getting married. Was that right?

Moral Rules are higher than laws. They are not religions but are adopted by every religion. Moral rules are the same for everyone, regardless of religion or race. And moral force is the strongest force there is! Furthermore, living by moral rules can lead you to peace. Go back to your religious books and learn moral laws. There is also a book on Moral Rules by the author.

CHAPTER 29: SELF-WORTH AND REJECTION

How you react to a rejection tells us how much you value yourself.

Are you going to kill yourself, kill the other person, hurt yourself, or hurt the other person?

If you value yourself and if you are "grown-up," you will accept the rejection, let it go, and make a new life for yourself.

Are we going to have contempt for you or admiration?

In life, you will meet many rejections in selection for schools, employment, promotions, services, sports, and so on. You may fail as an actor or in your business. You may be rejected by the person you are wooing, or after marriage, when he decides to love someone else. These scenarios are part of life.

The rejected person who has self-worth does not take these personally. He has the self-confidence that he can handle the rejection and survive.

He chalks it up to destiny, luck, or other reasons not in his control ("It happens!"). He shrugs it off and tries something else or another person. The important thing is that he does not take it personally or develop an inferiority complex. His self-worth holds him up. He knows he has the qualities to attract someone else or do something else to survive. He will see what can he learn from this.

He understands that this rejection does not mean that he is no good.

It may be that another candidate had what the selector was looking for or that the selector had a quota or other pressure. He may be a failure in business or acting, but he may be successful at something else. It may be that the person he is trying to woo is not attracted to him. That does not mean he is inferior. It just means that the chemistry did not click. So he shrugs it off and builds his life with someone else.

But to the person who knows he is no good, has no value and has an inferiority complex, the rejection is a personal insult.

He takes the rejection as a personal attack *since he has no other quality to feel good about.* So, he attacks the person rejecting him, or he kills himself.

He insists that the person or the position should belong to him alone. This is a sign of an inferiority complex.

Or he will try to feel powerful. **A person with an inferiority complex can only feel powerful by causing pain to others.** So he will throw acid on her face, disfiguring her and proving that he is a worthless piece of humanity.

He deserves the same done to him. This does not make us the same as him. His action was out of pure cruelty and malice. Our action is to act as a deterrent so that no one else dares copy his action. We are trying to protect society.

How you react to a rejection tells us how much you value yourself.

The woman whose husband is having an affair decides to kill herself to teach him a lesson or because she is angry, in pain, or in sorrow. She is not the first woman whose husband has been unfaithful. Why does that become a factor for self-destruction?

What lesson of courage does she leave behind for others? Why does she neglect her responsibilities to her children and her family?

Are her self-image and self-worth so fragile that another man can lead her to self-destruction?

The point is this: Why do you have such an inferiority complex? If you think you are good, you will consider the infidelity or rejection as an ultimate loss for the other party. Did you forget that you have so many wonderful qualities?

If your husband or friend has decided not to value you anymore, consider it his loss. Accept your freedom to live with dignity and show him that you can be happy without him and with self-respect.

You have forgotten that you have come to this earth to learn and develop. **The very purpose of rejection was to teach you something.** You were to learn the courage and inner strength that comes with living alone. But by killing yourself or the other person, you lose your education completely!

Why would you want someone to be forced to come to you against her will? Are you really such a terrible person that you have no hopes of getting anyone else or any other position by any other means?

The best revenge is to do better than your opponent.

Many a person, at the end of his life, can look back and finally understand why it was not meant to be, or even be grateful that he did not get what he wanted.

PART 7: OUR WEAKNESSES CAUSE EMOTIONAL PAIN

CHAPTER 30: DO YOU HAVE AN INFERIORITY COMPLEX?

You have no self-value when you have an inferiority complex. If you have an inferiority complex, you will be abused. A person gets an inferiority complex when his self-confidence is taken away. Inferiority complex also occurs if one has no skills or does not know how to behave. Or one may be conditioned to believe that one is no good.

When people want to control you, the first two things they do is take away your self-confidence and give you an inferiority complex. They laugh at your efforts and call you "stupid or no good."

The way to get out of the inferiority complex is to:

First, become financially independent.

Second, leave the people abusing you or taking away your self-confidence.

Third, develop self-value, self-care, self-respect, and self-protection.

Fourth, develop your self-confidence by doing things on your own. It is okay to make mistakes as long as you learn from them.

A person with an inferiority complex can only feel superior by making others feel inferior.

When one has an inferiority complex but no power, he becomes subservient and allows himself to be abused. But when he comes into power, he becomes intimidating, insulting, and abusive.

CHAPTER 31: ARE YOU A CHILD?

When we are not grown up, we cause ourselves emotional pain. Who is a child?

A child wants other adults to fix his problem while an adult handles his problems.

A child wants others to take care of him. An adult takes care of himself and also takes care of others.

However, one is also not grown up if one only takes care of others' physical welfare, not his own.

A child blindly follows the beliefs that others tell him. An adult thinks about whether the beliefs are right.

A child cannot live by himself. An adult can.

A child is told what to do. An adult takes charge of his life and decides where he wants to live, what work he wants to do, and who he wants to marry.

A child waits for you to tell him what to do when you are in a bad situation. The adult will decide for himself that you need help, what type of help, and will be there.

A child will act impulsively. An adult will act after seeing if it is in his interest, happiness, and long-term welfare to do so.

A child needs the approval of others. An adult does not.

A child will go back to the one who abuses him because he is dependent on them for love. An adult will not tolerate the abuse.

CHAPTER 32: FATHERS & EMOTIONAL PAIN

A man sometimes thinks that because he earns money, he automatically knows how to do parenting. He thinks that his money changes into knowledge in his brain. If this is true, then he should get a Ph.D. in many subjects without studying.

Then, he compounds his crime (and it is a crime) by refusing to let his wife give any input.

This becomes the cause of severe emotional pain in his children and generations after. The knowledge of parenting can only come from being taught or observing *good* parenting.

In such cases, the wife will have no option but to leave the home and the children or alienate herself from her children. Perhaps men and women should take a parenting test before the State.

The child is blessed when he has a father who is involved with the wellbeing of his child. He overcomes all temptations to stay married and give his child a stable home. **He invests time in his child**. He teaches character before sports. He teaches his child self-control, moral values, and character. He sees that his child has a happy home.

He does not struggle for power with his wife, nor does he demean her or contradict her to his children.

But at the other end of the spectrum are different types of fathers, all selfish. We will talk about some of those.

The first we will talk about is the father, who will abandon his responsibilities. He will walk away.

Second, he may stick around, but not physically. He makes money to leave for his child in the future. **However, he does not invest any time in his child.** He will not teach the child character, moral values, or self-control. He will not see if his child is unhappy and why. He will not go to the teacher or doctor to get input about his child. He will not see that his child is getting addicted, including to the phone. **He is guilty of not doing any parenting, and that is a crime.** In his old age, he wonders why he is so lonely.

The third type of father is so controlling that he will not allow the other parent to have any input in the raising of the child. He is greedy for power and may even be abusive to the other parent, ultimately forcing her to abandon her home and deprive the child of her love. Furthermore, he will completely alienate the child against her. The family falls apart. Even after he is long dead, the children will alienate themselves from their mother and each other.

There is the father who feels powerful by raising his children through constant fear of his punishment.

There is the father who will give his children the freedom to do anything they want as long as they stay with him. This selfish man is not interested in morality or character.

The courts have a hard time trying to protect the child from such parents and preventing the alienation of the other parent from the child.

To turn a child against the other parent is an emotional abuse of the child and is a legal crime. Any abuse leads to emotional pain.

CHAPTER 33: FALSE NOBILITY

There are two things that true nobility cannot allow you to be.

1. Nobility cannot allow you to become self-destructive.

But false nobility will. Do not sacrifice your happiness just to please others.

2. Nobility cannot allow you to become an enabler.

But false nobility will. By taking care of the welfare of abusers, you are enabling them to continue their abuse.

The first duty of a human being is to stop abuse in any house. Abuse is not a private affair. It is a social illness. It can only be stopped by making it public.

To tolerate situations where your self-respect, dignity, and reputation are attacked is "false nobility."

To care for those who do so, are unfaithful, or had abandoned you in the past is "false nobility." Do not do this, even if the alternative is loneliness. Because by doing this, you are showing that you have no self-value, self-worth, or self-respect. If you do not value or respect yourself, why would others?

In the end, you will become a shriveled, bitter person because your biggest hope that they will change their behavior has not been realized. Once a tree becomes crooked, you cannot change its shape. The same is true of character.

It is not your job to change anyone's character. And They will never change. The movies are lies.

It is also false nobility to put yourself in danger or unnecessary hardship when things can be accomplished in another way.

Cursing, making fun of others, demeaning, and insulting them is not freedom of speech.

*It is **"Verbal Abuse"** and is as painful as physical abuse.*

Verbal abuse must be punished as severely as physical abuse, with large fines and imprisonment.

CHAPTER 34: DO YOU ACCEPT ABUSE?

Do not control others!

Any contact with an abuser will give you lifelong emotional pain. Your only chance of survival is to get far away as fast as possible or to fight back for your rights.

An abuser wants you to live the way he would never accept for himself.

To prevent abuse:

You must, in advance, define **the length of time and the number of incidences** of abuse that you are willing to accept. (Not more than two instances and not more than three months).

Recognize abuse. Abuse does not have to be an active onslaught of pain. It can also be abandonment.

Accept that the abuser can be your parent, spouse, or child.

Do not mistake your lack of self-respect for nobility.

To stop abuse

Recognize abuse immediately when it occurs.

Give no excuse for the abuser. Would he accept such behavior from anyone? Would he excuse his employer if he were treated thus?

Never enable an abuser. Do not continue to excuse him, live with him, or not allow him to be punished under false nobility. He must be punished.

Do not have false hopes that he will "grow up" or change. This will never happen.

The more chances you give to an abuser, the worse the abuse will get.

Recognize an abuser. Leave an abuser.

Once you have left, you should speak to an abuser, *only through a third person or in front of others.*

Never walk out on an impulse!

Instead, carefully plan your departure, where you will go, how you will sustain yourself, and who will take care of your children while you work.

9. Understand that to the abuser, you are just *like a wine bottle is to an ex-alcoholic*. The temptation to slip back into his old behavior is irresistible. Stay away from him!

PART 8: KNOWLEDGE IS POWER

CHAPTER 35: UNCONDITIONAL LOVE

There are very manipulative people in our society who have come up with "terms" so that they can escape their responsibilities.

Since they do not want to become a better person, they hope that we will fall for their phrases. After all, who does not like to escape responsibility? But because of this, they have become responsible for a lot of emotional pain in our society. We need clarity about these phrases. Society has to hold them accountable for not fulfilling their responsibilities and many of them eventually land in jail.

Some of the phrases are

1. *"This is not who I am."* Did another spirit creep into his body? What he is saying is "Do not punish me. I do not want to be held responsible for what I did."

2. *"Parenting needs "quality time, not quantity.*" They say this to cover their guilt for being selfish and bad parents. To teach character to your child takes years. They say bonding is achieved by taking your child to the movies. Nothing could be further from the truth. This lie is the cause of all these teenagers who are in jail, as well as parental abuse and murders in the schools. Every animal gives all its time to its young ones to prepare them to handle life.

A parent who loves his child knows that parenting requires enormous time over many years to teach him character, moral values, life skills, self-control, and discipline.

3. Another phrase they have come up with is **"Unconditional love."**

This removes all responsibility on the part of a child or person to change his behavior and be a better person.

What they are saying is, "I am going to be as bad, as abusive, and as evil as I can. And I will get away with it because I have **brainwashed** you into thinking that you still have to love me and take care of me.

That is such an outrageous lie! Where then is the incentive to change? What happened to our duty to teach character, moral values, and self-control?

It is the duty of a parent to bring up upright, responsible, courteous, and law-abiding children.

Even the Bible says, "Spare the rod and spoil the child!" The Bible does not want you to spoil your child. If he does wrong, you are to punish him. If he is too big to be punished, you are to remove him from your life. He has to understand what is expected from him and accept the consequences of his abusive and irresponsible behavior. He has to be accountable.

Even God does not love us unconditionally! He will not love us if we act evil. You have to behave morally and treat him with reverence to get his love. He expects you to do the same with your children.

True love always has to be conditional!

Only then may he change.

Only then can you keep your self-respect.

Only then can you protect yourself and the other people in your life from abuse.

Only then can you show yourself to be a strong person with values.

Only then can you teach him self-control, which will lead him to inner strength.

CHAPTER 36: "EMOTIONAL BLINDNESS" & "THE PULSE"

Emotional blindness leads to emotional pain. So wrapped are we in our daily activities and ourselves that we are completely oblivious to how we are being treated and how others are feeling,

We do not see that we are not valuing our self-respect. We are not taking care of our welfare and our "Nine Healths." We tolerate abusive behavior in the name of "false nobility" or because this abusive family is all we have, and we are scared to be alone.

Or we do not see that our behavior is driving others away. We may be angry, controlling, abusive, non-caring, greedy, or selfish.

We are unaware of things occurring in front of us. Our fights are increasing.

Someone at home is hiding from us his behavior towards others.

Someone is manipulating us for selfish reasons. He does not care that this is causing us pain.

Someone is treating us the way he would never allow himself to be treated.

Someone at home is having psychiatric problems.

Our spouse is having an affair.

Our spouse has withdrawn all the money from our joint account.

Our child is becoming addicted to immoral programs with cruelty, hatred, and bad manners.

There is suicide in the making.

Our spouse is dividing our family instead of uniting it.

We do not see that contempt and hatred towards us are steadily growing.

We are being abused.

When the situation has reached its peak, and our house has burned down figuratively, we stand devastated. "How could I not see this?" we ask.

The answer is simple. We were emotionally blind.

We did not make the time and effort to check the "pulse of our home."

The "pulse of family life."

We have been taught that life is about taking care of our *daily activities* for survival and health. That means our office work, taking care of our family members, children, school work, and social life. It is also about education and taking care of our finances.

No one has mentioned the most vital one.

It is to keep our hand on the pulse of family life. This pulse is the current of all the emotions running through our home. It is a very vital current!

We cannot afford to shut off our radar.

We are alert to protect our family from outside forces. **Who tells us about what is happening inside***?* Our radar does. But we have shut off our radar!

Love and trust cannot be blind.

Our excuse is that we trust everyone loves us and everything is fine. But we cannot afford to be blind in our love and trust. We do not realize that home life requires constant checking, like a plant that will die from a lack of attention besides water.

We are emotionally blind for the following reasons.

1. We have no time.

We do not even *want* to spend the time checking the pulse of our home life. After all, we have a meeting tomorrow. There is a presentation to be made. The groceries must be bought, the dinner made, the children have a recital, the house needs to be cleaned, and the list goes on.

We will have lots of time afterward to regret that we did not make the time.

Anything we give our time to generally turns out fine. The dinner turned out okay. The children's recital went through. The presentation was appreciated at the office.

But "the pulse of our home" is being neglecte, and may be very sick.

2. We do not see the pattern.

We would rather take each hurtful act for *itself.* We will fight over it, react to it, cry, and start living our lives again. We do not see that it belongs to the same pattern of behavior.

How is our child behaving? Is he out of the pattern for his usual self? Is this how he behaved six months ago? Is he quieter?

There is a pattern of staying away, late nights at the office, dropping calls when you enter the room, and hanging up a phone call when you answer it. Be on alert.

3. We have wishful thinking.

We hope that the selfish or bad treatment by our spouse will stop. We hope that we will no longer be abused because he will grow up. Does a crooked tree become straight? Character, once formed, rarely changes. It is not your job to change the character of your spouse.

Schedule The Time

Give yourself fifteen minutes twice a week. Put away your phone and think about every family member. Is he happy, distant, different, sad, or evasive?

Sit with your family daily for twenty minutes or so and talk. See how they interact with each other and their attitude.

Spend ten minutes daily with each person individually *without* the TV, laptop, or iPhone, and give your full undivided attention.

Make the time. None of your other work is worth it if you lose your marriage or a child!

The most important thing to focus on your child is his character. It is not your taking him to football games or dancing school. The character of your child will determine whether he will turn around and abuse you, drop out of school, rape someone, go into school and shoot people, or commit suicide.

Make the time every week to read to your children a true story about someone who overcame depression and difficult times, who handled rejection and loneliness, or someone who showed courage, dedication, self-control, or wisdom.

Talk to your child about your beliefs and the purpose of life. Let him know what moral rules you believe in. You should read a book on moral rules to them from the early age of three.

Sometimes, you do not have to ask questions. Just start talking casually. Or you can tell a story about what your cousin, uncle, or grandparent did.

If your child has called you, take the time to listen to the pain in his voice. Ask if he is okay. Have a walk with him. Check on him if you think something is not right.

If your radar is beeping

Once you are suspicious, all rules go out of the window! Check the phone/ message log of the person concerned. Go through his drawers, bags, computer, etc. You are trying to save a life or a marriage here. Talk to his friends and (in your child's case) their parents. Go to a counselor/therapist. Get an investigator.

Hopefully, you were in time to save a marriage or a life.

CHAPTER 37: CANNOT RECOGNIZE A RELATIVE?

We put up with pain repeatedly from some people because they are our relatives. They will abandon us in our bad times, refuse to visit us or stay in contact, not carry their share of responsibilities, nor help us on social occasions but sit down as guests. And they have no gratitude for what we have done for them.

You have to fulfill the responsibilities of a relative to be considered one. A relative has to care. Caring means that he has to give his time and effort.

A relative stays in contact with you. He checks on you periodically to see whether you are alright and what he can do to help if you are not. He makes the time to come and visit you. Dropping a gift on your doorstep and leaving does not qualify him as a relative.

In times of need, he takes care of your welfare and the welfare of your family to the best of his ability. He is by your side to celebrate the good times and give help in the bad ones.

He does not have to be told to come. A child has to be told to come. He should do so automatically the minute he hears that his parent is ill or in distress.

Please beware of the person who says that he is busy and has no time to stay in contact or come to see you. This is the definition of selfishness. You do not need him in your life.

Those relatives who abandon you in time of need and then want to come back should be considered toxic. It is false nobility to take them back.

CHAPTER 38: CANNOT RECOGNIZE AN ENEMY?

We put up with tremendous pain for years because of our inability to recognize our enemy. He may be disguised as a parent, spouse, child, teacher, friend, relative, employee, or even our government.

Who Is An Enemy?

It is one who deliberately causes us pain and suffering and feels powerful by hurting us. He is selfish and unfair. He is non-caring about our pain. And he is immoral.

He makes us suffer so that he has security and pleasure.

He treats us as he would never tolerate being treated himself.

He will want us to live a life he will not accept for himself.

He will take our land. He will deny us the same freedom, rights, education, privileges, and benefits that he insists on for himself because we are women or from a different race, religion, or tribe.

And he will say he was provoked by the abused to do so.

He does not mind lying to hide his actions. He can only be controlled through fear. We can only get rid of our pain by leaving him or removing his power to hurt us.

PART 9: GET STRONG

CHAPTER 39: WHAT IF?

(NOTE: The following does not apply to abuse and physical suffering).

What if, for just one month, you ignore your emotional pain and live as if it does not exist?

What have you got to lose by acting this way?

What if you live drug-free for one month after tapering off all your anti-depressant medications?

Now you can think clearly!

What if you decide to go through the fire of your emotional pain without any anti-depressant or anti-anxiety medication?

You will come out stronger.

Let us see what happens for one year if:

You fail, but do not let it bother you. Instead, you calmly study again for the next examination.

Others will not give you what you want, so you decide to get it on your own.

You are unable to get married, so you join some matchmaking organizations. In the meantime, you continue to live happily.

You are not able to get or keep the person you love. You chalk it up to his bad luck and look forward to meeting someone better.

Your spouse is unfaithful. You leave him and decide to live on your own for now. You believe that he does not deserve a person as valuable as you. You decide this is your chance to see if you can get along without him.

You decide to try a different place for a year to see if you can handle being alone and the change.

You decide to love, take care of, and protect yourself as much as you do others.

You decide to make all the decisions for your welfare and happiness.

You decide to value work and money and support yourself financially.

You decide to practice self-discipline and meditation for one year.

You become interested in what is happening in the world.

You decide to have no communication with the ones who caused you pain.

You were treated poorly by the ones you love. You decide to remove them from your life and live on your own.

You lost a loved one and, after the mourning period is over, decide to have love again.

What if, for one year, you decide that the world is not such a bad place after all? If there are evil people, there are also people who are equally determined to love and help others and make it better for everyone. What if you decide to become one of those?

What if you understand that depression is an emotion?

Like any emotion, it can be substituted, displaced, or replaced by another emotion or even by pretending to have a happy emotion day after day.

What if you pretend to be happy and grateful for one year?

Well then, you become a person full of self-value, self-worth, self-respect, self-confidence, and self-discipline with a sense of purpose. Can you imagine such a being trying to kill himself? Of course not!

His self-worth does not come from his spouse, children, wealth, or status.

His self-worth comes from who he is. It comes from his day-to-day activities in which he offers caring, compassion, fairness, excellence in work, and independence in thought.

What if you decide that, for one year, you will leave the emotions that have caused you such pain by substitution, displacement, distraction, willpower, focus, meditation, and help from others?

And what if your greatest accomplishment this year is overcoming your emotions of anger, depression, fear, sadness, and self-destruction?

Wouldn't that be something?

CHAPTER 40: YOUR "FIFTEEN SELVES."

Before you separate, divorce, or commit suicide, it is crucial to know your "Fifteen Selves."

There are two "selves" that you must *not* develop: These are being selfish and self-destructive.

Some forms of self-destructiveness include being angry, having an addiction, not valuing your work, family, or money, not following moral rules, and doing whatever your emotions tell you without thinking of the consequences.

Self-destructiveness also includes suicide.

Selfishness is not to "care, share, or be fair." It means to only care about your pain, not the pain you will cause others.

Any teacher will tell you that a child entering school with self-value, self-respect, self-worth, self-confidence, and self-discipline is ahead of others!

But he can only develop these by the way you treat him and if you have these qualities yourself.

When you do not have your fifteen selves, you have deficiencies in your personality and will suffer a lifetime of emotional pain.

The Fifteen Selves.

1. Self-value

Lack of self-value causes pain. Throw away that inferiority complex. Do not believe anyone who says you are stupid or no good.

When you value yourself, you protect yourself financially. Money is power. Do not waste.

Rejection in love, job, or other situations does not decrease your value and is never to be responded to by violence to yourself or others. It is Nature's way of saying that "this is not for you." You should explore alternate ways. If you ignore this lesson, you will suffer again.

"Nature is such a good teacher that it will repeatedly expose us to similar situations until we learn our lesson." (Buddha).

2. Self-Care

For a year before you leave our world, take care of yourself as you would take care of a loved one.

3. Self-Worth

Your self-worth does not depend upon pleasing others, being loved, or acts of nobility!

It is very important to get your self-worth from multiple sources. Your self-worth will determine whether you will be abused or manipulated. Your self-worth will determine how you will handle a failure, rejection, or loss.

4. Self-Respect

Love that attacks one's self-respect is no love.

If one respects oneself, one does not tolerate disrespect or abuse, not even for maintaining peace or having a family.

Do not mingle with people who do not respect you and do not protect your reputation.

Being nice to an abuser is cowardice and shows a lack of self-respect.

5. Self-Confidence

To take away the self-confidence of a human being by demeaning him is a moral crime.

The first thing that people do to control you is to take away your self-confidence. They do this by saying that you are no good, stupid, or do not know how to behave. They are brainwashing you into thinking that you are no good.

Anyone who does this, whether parent, spouse, child, teacher, or employer, should be considered your worst enemy and be removed from your life.

The good news is that you can get your self-confidence back. You do this by achieving small victories first, understanding that it is okay to fail since you learn something from it, and being around people who value you.

6. Self-Reliance

Depend on yourself to get what you want, including education, a job, a car, or marriage. To ask others to give these to you makes you a child.

7. Self-Decisive

For one year take charge of your life. Make your own decisions. Do what is in the interest of your welfare and happiness but stay within your moral boundaries. Stop living your life as others want you to. Do not have the "disease to please." If you let others decide your life, you will suffer pain. Selfish people want you to fulfill their dreams.

But plan before you make any decision. There should be no impulsive decisions! *Failing to plan is planning to fail!"* Do not walk out of the house on impulse. Plan your escape from abuse. How will you support yourself? Where will you go?

8. Self-Sustenance

Support yourself financially or earn your keep. It adds to your self-respect.

9. Self-Protection:

Protect your safety, happiness, welfare, well-being, and future.

Protect yourself by having a moral boundary that you do not cross and an emotional boundary to keep toxic people out.

Protect yourself from **"Mob Mentality"**. Think for yourself.

Leave anyone who abuses you. Give only two chances. Get rid of your dependency on such people, otherwise you will kill yourself or have lifelong pain.

"You cannot heal in the environment that gave you pain." Buddha.

To do this, you need to keep your power.

Do not give away the power to make your own decisions for your welfare and happiness.

Do not give away your money to others. Money is power.

Do not give away your power of equal rights, education, financial independence, and social support.

The person who wants to control you will always want to take away these powers and your self-confidence.

Self-protection means recognizing your enemies.

Anyone who causes you pain and hardships is your enemy. One who loves you will not cause you pain.

Your enemy wants you to sacrifice your long-term happiness for his happiness.

He wants you to live the way he would not tolerate to live himself.

Anyone who takes away your self-confidence, abuses you, abandons you, ruins your reputation, and treats you with disrespect, cruelty, non-caring, and contempt is your enemy.

Anyone who denies you the freedom, rights, and benefits that he wants for himself is your enemy.

Anyone who tells you that you cannot be educated or prevents you from praying the way you want is your enemy.

10. Self-Discipline

Without self-discipline, you are a weakling being swayed by your emotions like a puppet on a string. Self-discipline gives you great inner strength. You are in control!

Self-discipline means doing what you do not want to do.
For example, you may not want to wake up early in the morning
daily, but you force yourself to do so.

Self-discipline and self-control are physical and mental.

11. Self-Control

Self-control means not doing what you want to do. Self-
control of emotions is critical. It is a sign of personal development.
Self-control starts with practicing good manners at home and
treating others with respect.

Delaying gratification, not having what you want
immediately, is an essential type of self-control.

Do not control others.

12. Self-Planning:

Plan your life to avoid making impulsive decisions and
suffering pain.

Plan to live for a year at your highest level! See the chapter,
"The Critical Year" in this book.

13. Self-Strength

This is also called "inner strength" and differs from the
strength and encouragement that others give you. This comes from
your inside. This strength will help you to go forward when every
fiber of you wants to quit.

It is to fight by yourself, your pain, anguish, terror, demons,
and your addiction to people as well as to chemicals.

14. Self-Knowledge

Think about the following questions: What is causing you pain? What can you do about it? What type of person are you? What are your weaknesses? What is your strength? What type of a person do you wish to be?

15. Self-Improvement

This requires humility and the ability to learn from anyone, including a beggar or a child.

These fifteen aspects are part of our development and lead us to self-confidence, inner strength, and peace.

END OF SECTION ONE

SECTION TWO

SUICIDE

Do you want to kill yourself?

Before you commit suicide, you should visit someone who has lost a loved one through suicide.

See the lifelong pain you will cause to your loved ones.

Who causes pain to the ones they truly love?

PROLOGUE

The World Health Organization estimates that about one million people die from suicide each year, representing a global mortality rate of 16 people per 100,000 or one death every forty seconds. Suicide is the second leading cause of death among those from 15 to 25 years old.

This statistic represents tremendous pain, anguish, and despair among us. Suicide is committed across all walks of life. What can be done to decrease this awesome loss of human potential? These are intelligent, talented people! These are people capable of deep love and caring for humanity. How can they be convinced that they are truly worthwhile people who can contribute so much to the human race?

Who can blame them for ongoing physical pain and suffering, poverty, abuse and injustice, and the loss of freedom and the benefits that are enjoyed so carelessly by the rest of us?

But what about situations with a chance for change? What if a change was happening a year or so from now? What if they could be convinced to stay around long enough to see it?

When pain is emotional, it can test the soul, teach the soul, and help it change and grow. Sensitivity arises out of suffering. If so, then truly, these people are sensitive to the pain of others. They have empathy. The corollary, then, is that they can help others besides themselves. That makes them essential people to have around.

In the following pages, an approach to preventing suicide has been presented. Knowledge is power and can lift the darkness of emotional pain. The pain has arisen from emotions.

It is by controlling our emotions that we develop and grow. This requires time.

CHAPTER 41: THE CHECKLIST

A. Fill in your answers on a sheet of paper to the statements below and review them in thirty days.

I do not want to live because:

____

____

Life is too painful.　　( ) Yes. ( ) No.

I understand that this pain is a feeling and that feeling is an emotion.　　( ) Yes. ( ) No.

I know that I am supposed to control my emotions. They are not supposed to control me.

( ) Yes. ( ) No.

I have tried to seek help from people who can alleviate my pain.　　( ) Yes. ( ) No.

I have spoken to someone about this.

( ) Yes. ( ) No.

If not, because___________________________

I understand that I should wait until I grow up to kill myself, or if I am an adult, I have explored all my options, including the fact that things may improve with time.
( )Yes. ( ) No.

I have a dependency on a person/persons.

( )Yes. ( ) No.

I have a dependency on drugs/substances.

( ) Yes. ( ) No.

I cannot face the world because I am ashamed of my child or parent.

( )Yes. ( ) No.

I cannot control his actions. I understand that my identity has to be separate from his.

( ) Yes. ( ) No.

I place a high value on myself.

( ) Yes. ( ) No.   If not, why not?---.

I know that after I die, I do not just disintegrate. I still exist. I will meet the reception committee. I will have to explain my actions and accept the consequences.   ( ) Yes. ( ) No.

I acknowledge that I do not know how much *more pain* I will have in the other world because of my suicide. ( ) Yes. ( ) No.

I know I have been sent to this earth, not as an accident, but with a specific purpose to develop myself.   ( )Yes. ( ) No.

This includes the courage to handle life.

( ) Yes. ( ) No.

My thought of suicide is on an impulse because I cannot have someone I love/someone who has rejected me. ( ) Yes. ( ) No.

I understand that I will not have this person after death either, so what am I achieving by dying?

    b. I am angry at someone.   ( ) Yes. ( ) No.

    c. I did not get what I wanted. ( ) Yes. ( ) No.

I understand that these are emotions. I know that acting on an impulse is not part of being grown-up.

                        ( )Yes. ( ) No.

Date .------------

Date .------------ (After 30 days).

If all the pupas killed themselves, there would be no butterflies!

CHAPTER 42: WHERE DO YOU GO AFTER SUICIDE?

Where will you go after you kill yourself? It is so easy to die: You pull the trigger or the noose or swallow some pills, and you are gone.

But gone where? What world have you entered?

Your journey has just begun.

Most people limit their thinking to the point of death and stop there. Why?

Why do you not focus on what happens next?

You have entered a world from which you cannot turn back, even if you now decide to. Suddenly, you are no longer in control. You are completely helpless! You are told what to do and where to go. On earth, you had choices. In the next world, you have none. Think about that.

Your personality existed before you were born.

You came to this earth with distinct personality traits and unique gifts. For example, you may paint well while another person is inclined to take up sports. You may have a talent for writing or music. You may design better. You may have a gift for languages.

Where did you get these traits and gifts?

You have also come to this earth at different levels of development. You may be more or less calm or angry, selfish or caring, patient or impatient, and so on. You may have the qualities of a leader. You may have courage, including the courage to face life, while another person may be a coward.

How did you reach your level of development?

Does your personality die when the body dies?

You existed before you were born. This is why you came here with certain individual traits and development. Then it follows that you cannot disappear into "nothing" when you die. You go back to the place that you came from.

What happens after you die?

Do you think that, after you die, you become a piece of dust? Of course not! You leave your body to go forward in the afterlife to meet your Creator and teachers.

And they have some questions to ask you!

What will you show them about what you learned on Earth? Did you complete what you were sent to this earth to learn? What if you deliberately "dropped out of school" by killing yourself?

You are not once thinking about whether, at the other end, there will be a welcoming committee to greet you or an angry or disappointed one because of what you have done.

Some of the unhappiest souls are those who commit suicide.

What if you continue to have pain and suffering in the other world? What will you do then?

After all, you cannot kill yourself there. You are already dead! How, then, did your suicide help?

If you can be sent to Earth the first time, do you not think that you can be sent right back?

If you had been sent to Earth to learn, you might be sent right back to complete your course. Perhaps you will exist as a ghost to finish your designated time on Earth. You will watch helplessly as your loved ones suffer.

Is this what you want?

CHAPTER 43: QUESTIONS YOU WILL BE ASKED AFTER DEATH.

After you die, you will meet your Maker and be asked the following questions. Why not prepare your answers before you go?

1. Did it justify giving your loved one "lifelong" emotional pain when you could not handle your emotional pain even for another week?

2. When you love someone, you protect them from pain. Here, you gave them pain instead! Then how can you love them? You did not once care how the family would survive after you were gone. You deprived your family of the love, protection, and care that you alone could provide. Is this only about you? Is that not selfish?

3. What provisions did you make before departing to take care of your parents when they grew old and weak? What provisions did you make for your children or your dependents? Or did you only think about yourself?

4. What will happen to your child when he lacks the love, protection, and guidance that only you, as his parent, could have given him? You are then responsible for his suffering!

You have violated a child's moral right to have his parent.

5. If you are willing to accept the pain of the afterworld's punishment, why did you not accept the pain on earth?

6. How do you know that your punishment here in this afterlife will not be more horrific? At least on earth, you could have absolved your sin through penance.

7. If you were depressed, why did you not seek help from others? Why did you not pray for guidance?

8. Why have you left your development unfulfilled? You will probably have to go right back to earth to learn the lessons you did not learn.

9. If you were haunted by your past, why did you not redeem it by your actions toward others?

10. If you were assaulted, why did you allow what others did to you limit your growth on earth?

11. What example did you leave to others in handling failure?

12. If the world was not perfect, what did you do to make your corner better?

13. If you left because the world was not to your liking, why did you not seek guidance from the One who sent you here? A lot of thought was spent on creating your soul. Why waste it?

14. Who said that you had to judge yourself by what others think of you, or if they reject you? They are made blind by their emotions.

15. If you suffered a loss, does not everyone have a loss? Was it not part of your test?

16. If you committed suicide because of emotional dependency, did you try to shake off your dependency on your loved one and live on your own for a year? Did you try to face the loneliness? Did you not think that you would miss him in the afterlife?

You left him anyway when you killed yourself. So why did you not try living without him for a year on earth?

17. If it was because of what others forced you to do in this life, why did you not leave them, become financially independent, and take charge of your life?

How could you consider them yours if they caused you pain for their pleasure?

18. Why did you kill others when you took your own life?

You cannot carry a gun into the other world. The Beings there are more powerful than you. Did it occur to you that they may not like anger, cruelty, and violence? To enter their world in a state of pain, anger, and violence will not help you, but it will upset those who receive you there. Do you want to do that?

19. You cannot justify your actions by saying that you blindly followed orders from your superiors. You are not supposed to follow orders blindly. Your superiors are not by your side in the other world to protect you!

The Laws of Humanity are above all of the laws of the world.

20. What redeeming qualities do you have? How much courage, compassion, and fairness did you develop before you left the earth? Can you show that you helped someone or made a difference, no matter how minute it was? Was your compassion restricted to your family, tribe, religion, or nation?

Would you rather sit in front of the committee that reviews your file *after your death* and be able to say the following? "Sirs, I lived my life to the best of my ability with the knowledge and the skills that I possessed. I followed your moral laws and controlled my emotions. I helped people and animals along the way, and I tried to fight against injustice."

Or are you going to say the following? "I did not care about Your moral Rules. I did not care about my responsibilities to my family. I did not care about the pain I was going to cause to everyone because I was only focusing on my own pain."

Do you know that suicide is a selfish act?

The act is selfish because you are only concerned about yourself.

You do not think about the lifelong pain you will give to completely innocent people: your children, your parents, and many others.

It is only about you and your pain.

Only when you have met your responsibilities to everyone and have tried everything you could to relieve your pain, and only when you are facing a future of suffering, physical or mental (with no cure or relief), should you think about suicide!

CHAPTER 44: THE COSMIC LAWS ON SUICIDE

Moral Rules are Cosmic Laws.

Do not confuse moral rules (ethics) with religion.

Moral laws transcend all religions but are adopted by each of them because they are fundamental to protecting our society and the individual in it. Also, they guide an individual to develop to his highest level.

Everything on this earth has laws governing it. Seasons follow each other. Day follows night. Each species in the animal kingdom has its life span. The plants obey Cosmic Commands, as does the field of genetics. It follows that suicide, too, must be governed by Cosmic Laws.

The Sixteen Cosmic Laws on Suicide

1. Do not commit suicide immediately.

Suicide is a milestone, and no milestone should be decided in a highly emotional state, be it marriage or death.

Take a month to decide. In this month, do the following.

a. You have thought about the pros and cons of your suicide.

b. You have discussed it with at least one other person.

Be sure that you can prove to the committee that meets you after your death that you had no other choice.

2. Suicide generally is immoral, but the following are the cases where suicide can be condoned:

physical cruelty,

untreatable, severe physical pain,

complete physical dependency,

relentless, progressive, debilitative illness from which there is no cure,

mental deterioration from which there is no cure,

unending loneliness,

lifelong bondage,

facing a terrible ending for oneself and

facing a painful way of life from which there is no possible relief. This includes a life of shame.

3. You must not commit suicide if you have a child, an elderly parent, or other beings who are dependent on you.
You cannot pass on this responsibility.

4. First, know your fifteen different selves.

Before you contemplate suicide, you must be aware of your fifteen different selves as part of your personal development. Read the chapter on them.

5. You must not kill another human being when you kill yourself unless it is to defend a person or your country.

You will compound your sins of suicide with homicide!

God is the Creator of life. What we create, we value. Therefore, since He creates life, He values life. He never gave you permission to be the "destroyer of life." You may feel powerful at this moment, but what happens when you die and meet the One whose law you just broke? Be very scared of entering your afterlife after such an action.

6. Suicide is never to be committed to express your emotions of anger and frustration.

This completely nullifies what your Creator has sent you here for.

Control of anger and frustration is part of the development you are sent to this earth to achieve.

Suicide is never to be committed because you did not achieve something that your heart was set upon.

First, you are not supposed to get whatever you want.

Second, it is sometimes by not getting what you want, that you develop.

Third, you may get something far better by not getting what you want.

Fourth, to think only of your disappointment and not your responsibilities to others is the height of selfishness.

7. Suicide is never to be committed because you failed at something.

Failing at something does not make you a failure. It is how you respond to failure that counts!

Part of the development that you are sent here to achieve is to handle failure, learn from it, and then get up and go forward. It does not necessarily mean that you try the same thing again. It means that you persist in developing. You will put your energy toward seeing what else you can do to the best of your ability.

8. Do not commit suicide because you are being forced to do something against your wish.

Suicide is not to be committed because your parents or others are putting too much pressure on you to perform well in studies, sports, or other activities. It is not to be committed because your parents want you to accept a career, a marriage, or go where you do not want to go. So, why not refuse, go on strike, or escape instead of killing yourself?

Figure out a solution. It does not matter if you lose the year in school. It is better to lose the year than to lose your life. Growing up means taking charge of your life and making your own decisions about your welfare and happiness.

First, it is abuse for any human being, including your parents, to ask you to be in pain so that they can have pleasure.

Second, though they may insist they push you for your benefit, they only do it for themselves.

Third, no parent should put the burden of his dreams on his child. If a parent cannot fulfill his own dreams, then he should accept this.

Each individual comes onto this earth with his own talents, gifts, and dreams to fulfill.

He does not need the additional burden of a parent's dreams.

It is a wise parent who lets his child develop his own talents and dreams. Can you imagine if Gandhi had to fulfill the dream of his brother or Mandela had to fulfill the goals of his mother, or Michelangelo had to fulfill the dream of his relatives? The world could never have improved!

On the other hand, you, the child, have no business wasting your parent's money if your interest lies elsewhere. However, you have the responsibility of earning enough to feed yourself and support your family, your dependents, and your parents. If you can do this by whatever grades you were getting in school or other acquired skills, then that is fine.

9. Suicide is not to be committed either because you did not get another person's love or because you lost it.

Your first lesson on earth is to love and value yourself as much as you do another.

Your second lesson is the ability to let go of the one you love.

Suicide is never to be committed because someone you love has left you or because your husband left you for another woman or betrayed your trust. The fact that he has been unfaithful does not end your world.

To face rejection and face life alone is part of the tests you must pass to develop.

You will be rejected at various stages in life. The devastation you feel should be slowly replaced by acceptance and focusing on your life and development.

When you have a loss from rejection and stop taking care of yourself, or you want to kill yourself, then what are you telling the person who has rejected you? Are you not saying that you are worthless without him and that life is only worth living because he is in your life? How can you believe that?

What has happened to your self-value and self-respect? Did you not exist before this person came into your life, and quite happily, too? And that was based on your self-worth! Why are you increasing his sense of self-importance?

Suicide is never to be committed to punish those who treated you badly or to make them feel guilty.

You are never to punish others by hurting yourself.

Suicide is never to be committed if your children leave you and stay with your ex-spouse because you never know when they will need you. Your spouse may face hard times or die.

10. Suicide is not to be committed because you have lost everything and will now face bad times.

Bad times teach us, while good times test us.

You may not develop much while you have everything. In good times, you can become non-caring, complacent, rude, arrogant, insensitive, unfair, addicted to pleasure, and even immoral.

It is in suffering that you become sensitive to the suffering of others. It is in bad times that you learn to control your emotions of anger and arrogance. In bad times, you think of how to exist and why you should do so. It is in bad times that you ask about the purpose of life and the reason for your existence.

If you wish to escape this world because you have no peace, rest assured that you will not get it in the next world. You are to attain peace here!

11. Suicide is not to be committed because you do not like yourself.

This is your chance to change yourself. People will commit suicide when their evil deeds are brought to light, and they know that they will be reviled by everyone on this earth. No one can stop them, but they should understand the type of reception they will get in the other world. You have to change yourself on earth.

12. Suicide is never to be used as a form of protest.

People who were too selfish to care while you were alive will not care enough to be shocked for long after you are gone. Nothing will change, and you will have wasted your life for nothing. You must value your life and the chance that you have been given to develop.

13. Suicide is not to be committed to promoting your cause.

First, it is a cowardly act. Second, it is not the way to achieve your goal. In fact, you may not even achieve your goal. Third, it smothers your development.

14. You must not kill yourself in a place of prayer, a church, a temple, a synagogue, etc.

These are places of communication with God, and He will not tolerate your making them a scene of disturbances. Do not compound your sin before meeting Him in your afterlife.

You must never kill another in a place of worship, even if his religion is different from yours.

15. You must never combine suicide with mass murders.

You do so because you are angry and want revenge, to please your masters, or to make someone feel momentarily afraid. Perhaps you want to go out with a "bang." But who will remember you after six months? Who will remember you with love? But they will certainly remember you with anger and disgust, if at all. Their feelings will not help you in the next world.

16. Suicide is never to be committed as a "mob mentality" or because others are doing it.

To commit suicide to bring death and destruction to helpless, innocent beings is a very grave sin. The last act that you do on this earth before you meet your Maker should not be that of the senseless killing of innocent beings. You are leaving pain and suffering behind in His world. Do you not think He will be angry?

Be very scared of facing Him. You will suffer tremendously in the next world.

Should you commit suicide if you are raped?

The answer is a "yes" if you are a child or adult *facing* a life of rape because you are imprisoned, in a brothel, or are sold for this purpose and have no avenue of escaping this horrible life.

The answer is an unequivocal "no" if you are a child or an adult who *has been* raped. You have been able to escape from the horrifying circumstances. It is the same as asking if you should commit suicide because a thief broke into your house. It is not your fault. The crime is his.

First, it is a sin of the person who committed the assault, so you have nothing to be ashamed of.

Second, anyone who thinks that, because of someone's assault, you are no longer a lovable person has no intelligence. A wise person knows that your identity and value have nothing to do with the behavior of any other person. Suppose a thief came into your home and beat up your husband. Would your husband then be no longer lovable?

Third, it is your duty to bring him to justice so that neither he nor others dare to repeat this act.

Fourth, do not feel sorry for yourself. It is an assault. Assaults will happen as long as there are evil people around. The question "Why me?" can never be answered, neither in this case nor in the case of someone getting cancer. Instead, your emotions should be of acceptanc*e* for what the assailant is: a worthless, evil coward! Also, you must get angry: "How dare he?" He needs to be punished severely.

It is a development to progress from "How could he?" to "How dare he!"

Fifth, conquer your past. Yes, he terrorized you. Yes, it is a traumatic memory, but development means not letting your past conquer you.

You must conquer your past, not let your past conquer you.

Sixth, in development, it is not what the others did to you that is important. It is how you react to it. That is important.

Perhaps you can join an organization of rape victims or other women's organizations that together can bring about changes in laws for rape and the necessary death penalty for the rapist. A girl was gang-raped at fifteen years of age in India. On growing up, she formed an organization, "Prajwala," that has rescued over seven thousand raped girls and children and helped to rehabilitate them.

CHAPTER 45: LETTER TO A SUICIDAL YOUTH

This is a letter to any child or teenager planning to kill himself (everything in this book applies equally to boys and girls).

Hello, My Dearest One,

You are feeling very sad, alone, and helpless today. You have an immense sadness in you, which makes it a burden to carry on living. No one understands the pain or fear in your heart.

Who would you be if your current emotions and circumstances did not overcome you? What could you not accomplish? But you cannot see this because you are covered by a blanket of despair.

May I talk things over with you for just a few minutes? You are going to say that I am trying to prevent you from killing yourself. Well, I am trying to understand your reasons only so that we can stop others like you, from killing themselves.

A lot of work was done by your Creator to bring you from a tiny, helpless baby to where you stand today. As a child, you learned to walk by yourself without caring what others thought.

You did not care how many times you fell until you learned to walk. There was no fear.

What happened to that spirit today?

Why do you care how many times you fall, or fail?

Have you forgotten the joy of independence that you would get in the end?

Do not commit suicide to make your loved ones feel guilty. They will not learn from it. Your life is too precious. You can be as effective by leaving them once you grow up.

You would have left them anyway if you killed yourself!

Is poverty bothering you? You suffer cold, poverty, and hunger. You have no shelter. You have to beg for food.

Is it difficult to learn? Many of us found it difficult to learn new things in the beginning. You can search the internet to find some programs to help with your education.

Do people avoid you because you have emotional outbursts when frustrated? Are you rude to others or people with authority? One of the ways to stop this is to count to ten before you respond. Or, you can keep quiet and respond after a whole day to calm down. You can decide that you will first learn to control your temper before you depart.

Maybe you are lonely. Your mother abandoned you. You have no friends or no real home.

To not have a single person who cares about you is very painful.

Seek social services or a part-time job to meet people. Can you ask for help from your school?

You may be lonely, but you are not alone in your position. So many others have been where you are today. They stood at the threshold of death with the same pain. But they did not take the next step and are thankful for it today. There is so much that they have learned by staying alive. And they have then channeled their pain to help others like them.

Adults do make mistakes. The question is how to survive until you reach adulthood and financial independence.

One of the things you are feeling is helplessness.

Did you know that one of our Presidents was very poor? He had no mother and no schooling. So he had to teach himself to read. Yet, he became the president of our country! This is because he had a goal to learn as much as possible. He was also hardworking and used his free time to do odd jobs for others. His name was Lincoln.

However, there can be other causes besides learning disorders as seen below:

You always have to compensate for the fact that you are a girl.

You failed your examination.

Your social life at school is causing you pain.

You are bullied at school.

You constantly fear being beaten, raped, or sexually abused. You are cursed and beaten.

You have no freedom to go anywhere. You are locked up with no access to the outside world. You have been sold or sent to work in another country to earn for your family and have no resources or help to return.

You are engaged in child labor. So you are made to work beyond the norms for your age.

Abandonment

You have been abandoned as a baby or as a child.

You were given up for adoption.

Adoption is the sign of ultimate rejection and is very painful.

You are in a foster home, shunted from home to home, and never allowed to stay in one place and bond with anyone.

Loss

Your mother died in childbirth, and your parent holds you responsible and refuses to see you. This is not your fault. But, it is immoral on the part of the parent.

There is the death of one or both parents. You are shunted from relative to relative because your parents are gone. You are separated from your siblings.

There is a divorce, and the parent you love so much has moved out of your home.

The court does not allow you to stay with the parent you love.

The court allowed your parent to alienate you from the other parent, and now you are consumed with hatred toward him. But now you do not understand why you are so unhappy!

Homelife

Because of your illegal activities, your parents do not want you in their home.

Your parent is selfishly absorbed in his addiction. He may be an alcoholic.

Your parent is selfishly absorbed in his own life or vocation and has no time for you.

Your parent does not protect you from abuse by the other parent.

Your parents treat you differently from the other children. You are the scapegoat.

You are not loved or are treated with anger because you remind your parent of the other parent. This is not your fault. This is wrong and immature on the part of your parent.

Your parent has remarried and has his own life. He has no time for you, and you have no room there.

When you go and live with the parent you love, you find that your parent is absorbed with his new family. So, you feel that you do not belong there.

Whichever parent's home you are in, there is criticism of your other parent, which hurts you deeply.

Low self-esteem

Your parents are alive, and you live with them, but they have marked contempt and constant anger towards you, no matter what you achieve.

You are repeatedly told that you are no good and worthless. Your efforts are made fun of. You are compared to your siblings, who are better achievers.

You are told that you are a burden on the family, perhaps because you are a girl.

Your parents love you and treat you well, but you have brought disappointment to your family because of your poor performance in your studies.

You have low self-esteem because your colleagues passed, but you have failed.

You have brought shame to your family because of your other activities.

You failed

Do you feel that you are a failure? But you learned something from that failure, didn't you? You will do things differently now. Failure is often a teacher in disguise.

Your failure does not define you.

It is your reaction to failure that defines you.

How often have we seen that the brilliant ones, who did so well in their studies, burn out quickly and do not contribute much to society? It is the slow, plodding ones who affect the world.

Are you addicted? Have you tried to overcome your addiction? Can you give yourself one year to get free?

Dear One, I hope that I have not missed anything. I do not deny the intensity of your pain.

Here are some suggestions.

Escape physically

A physical escape means that you can run away, but how far can you go without money? Do you have a relative or a teacher who you can visit periodically?

Have a goal

Keep yourself focused on your future when you will be independent of all this and when you can make a difference to others.

Seek Guidance

It helps to talk over things with an adult you can trust. She has some things that you lack. They are called experience, insight, and independence. She may be able to do something about your situation, or she may be able to give you an insight into how to handle it.

If you are a girl, talk to a woman. If you are talking to a man, understand that seeking advice does not give him the right to touch you or take advantage of you. Make sure that you do not meet this person, a man or woman, in a lonely place or at his or her apartment. You can talk in a park, coffee shop, in front of a store, or on the outside school grounds.

In some countries, schools have counselors, and there are suicide hotlines that you can call. You might talk to your teacher, a doctor, or a nurse in a hospital that you feel is caring. But again, the same rules apply. Do not meet them in an isolated place or at their homes. No matter how much you trust someone, stay away from places where you can be molested or locked up.

Talk things over

Talking things over with your peers does not help where guidance is concerned because they do not have the wisdom to guide you. *But you can still benefit from their caring, understanding, and sympathy.* The fact that you can unburden yourself also provides quite a relief. You are no longer alone. Someone cares about how you feel.

Keep your brain free from alcohol and addiction.

You need clarity of vision about what is happening and how you should react. This cannot be done by keeping your brain numb with addiction.

Do not fulfill your parent's dream.

You are not supposed to fulfill your parents' dreams. It is a selfish parent who insists that his child fulfills his dreams. Each person comes to this earth with his gifts, talents, and needs to fulfill his own dreams.

Seek Help

In case of cruelty or physical assault, approach adults, your teacher, your doctor, or the police.

In case of sexual assault, you are not guilty of anything. A male is looking at your naked body, touching your body, kissing you, or touching your private parts. This is wrong, but it is he who is wrong! It is not your fault. This is abuse. He knows that. This is why he will tell you not to tell anyone. But you must immediately inform an adult.

Most sexual assaults are committed by someone you know or in the family. If your mother does not protect you, then you must tell an outsider. This can be your teacher or your doctor but see that the person you tell is a woman.

Give it time

You do *not* give time to behaviors like physical assault, molestation, or imprisonment. They must be dealt with immediately.

But give yourself a year or two to failures, rejections, loss, pain, and loneliness. Focus on becoming strong. Overcome your emotions through self-discipline.

Do not let your present overwhelm you.

This too shall pass and before you know it you will be an adult in charge of your life and able to do things your way.

But we must acknowledge a few things here.

Youth is the time when our bodies are changing. Our emotions are churning, our hormones are still trying to find their rhythm in which to settle, and our brains are growing. We are growing in every direction. It is enough if we come through this intact.

What we do not need is another distraction.

A physical attraction, a love affair, will cause more havoc in our lives. And we do not need any type of addiction to complicate our life, be it alcohol, drugs, or sexual indulgence. There is enough turbulence inside us right now. We have to attain our height and growth, our hormones have to settle down into their right pattern, and we have to form our moral, ethical, and emotional boundaries.

Youth is a time of unsureness. Youth is the time when we are still looking for clarity of vision in our lives. We do not know why we are here, what it means to grow up, or how we are supposed to react to situations, people, or anything. Add to this the pain that we have because of our family or others.

We do not know what we want. If we do get what we want, we may find out that it is not really worth it. An example is when you get the boy you wanted to marry, but now you have to sacrifice your schooling, career, or wealth because of this.

We have two enemies: the ones without and the ones within. The ones within are our emotions.

Youth is the time when our emotions have us completely in their control.

Becoming strong

Becoming strong means that we control our emotions and not vice versa. This is done every day when we refuse to listen to them. If our emotions say that we are no good, we say that we are good. If the emotions say that we are bad because we failed, we say that we will try again or we will try something else. If our emotions say that we should kill ourselves, we will say no.

Self-control and self-discipline are the keys to becoming strong.

Here are two rules that can help you.

1. Do not stop at suicide.

Think about what will happen **after** you enter the next world. What if the beings there send you right back to earth?

2. Before you kill yourself, give yourself one year.

You can always die after that. You would have shown those in the afterlife that you tried your best.

Yes, you have tremendous pain, but you will get through it. Every day, you are growing and learning and becoming stronger. What you must not do is allow this pain to make you hate others.

Remember

It is the youth who are sensitive to problems in our society.

It is the youth who will defend our nation.

It is the youth who start the momentum to bring about changes in our society for the better.

It is the youth who will show the courage that sometimes adults will lack.

You have what the rest of us lack!

CHAPTER 46: SUICIDE IS NOT A PSYCHIATRIC ILLNESS

Do not transfer an attempted suicide to a psychiatric ward.

A person who has attempted suicide has done so because he is unhappy with his situation in life. He is in pain and has thought through the situation.

But that does not mean that he is crazy or psychotic.

The current tendency for hospitals to transfer patients to a psychiatric ward after they have attempted suicide is wrong and dangerous.

It must be stopped!

It causes further mental trauma to a patient who is already under severe emotional strain. In forty years of experience, the author did not find one potential suicide who was crazy. Suicide can be considered wrong, but wanting to kill oneself does not make a person automatically crazy. Highly intelligent, clear-thinking people have taken their lives.

Do not bring a psychiatrist into the picture. Do not transfer a suicidal person to a psychiatric ward. Do not think that, by doing this, you are absolving yourself of any responsibility.

On the contrary, you are adding to the problem.

Bring a priest or a counselor instead to provide sympathy and advice to the patient, and then let him go home. Your psychiatric ward cannot prevent him from attempting the act again.

The government should not make attempting or committing suicide a crime. When it is no longer a crime, people who have attempted suicide will not be afraid to seek help. People who have committed suicide have left our world in a great deal of pain. What are we achieving by attaching a stigma to their names?

CHAPTER 47: A PARTICIPATION IN CRIME

Those who do not report a planned suicide or homicide are as guilty as the ones committing it. They must be punished.

This does not apply to a medical-assisted suicide for a non-functional and deteriorating life with no treatment. It is unacceptable for any human being to live that way.

The worst person is the one who encourages the person to take his life. That is an evil act. He cannot hide behind the excuse for not thinking.

No matter which religion we belong to (or whether we are atheists), moral and legal laws apply to each of us. Furthermore, we all have a conscience that we must listen to. Other than children, justice demands that maximum punishment be applied to those guilty of keeping quiet, encouraging, and participating in such acts.

To apologize after being caught for the deed cannot mitigate your crime. You are not safe to be left loose in society.

Doctors and nurses, be aware that no "doctor-patient confidentially" can exist when someone is planning suicide.

In the case of a confession to a priest, the same rule applies. If the priest does not report the crime or the intention of committing it, he is equally guilty of the murder.

Above any contract of confidentiality with another person is the value of life. It is one's duty to prevent death from happening and preventing a recurrence.

CHAPTER 48: BEREAVEMENT OF A SUICIDE

Grief and bereavement are dealt with extensively in another book, but in death by suicide, there are some notable differences from other situations. Regardless of what they are, the deceased must be given the same type of rituals and cremation/burial as a non-suicide would get in his family.

The Differences are:

1. Shock.

The total unexpectedness of this parallels death by accident, except for one fact. This was planned. Yet, no warning was given to the ones who cared the most.

2. Guilt.

The guilt of not picking up any sign *immediately.*

Hints had been given that we were unable to recognize. For example, there was a phone call earlier that we presumed was an innocent one. Or, in our hurry, we did not wonder at the tone, the brevity of words, or the way the goodbye was spoken.

There is the guilt of not picking up signs *earlier.* We did not see this coming.

We pushed him too far in his studies.

We did not pay attention when he said he was unhappy.

We were only interested in having him do what we wanted.

We did not teach him to handle the difficult times in life.

We did not give him self-worth, self-value, or self-confidence.

We could not prevent him from falling into bad company or using drugs.

3. Shame.

We withdraw from society. "What must people be thinking about us?"

4. Neglect of other children.

We are so focused on the deceased that we do not realize that our other children, too, can commit suicide! This has happened!

5. Anger at the deceased.

We are angry at him for being selfish and not thinking about the pain and welfare of others.

One must admit that suicide is a selfish act!

Lack of peace.

You may have been the cause of the suicide, or you may not have. The fact remains that the deceased is not at peace, and you are not at peace. If you consider the deceased to still exist in another realm, then it is vital to help him find peace. The fact that he does exist is comforting. This is why people attend seances.

Find peace for the deceased and yourself

Do three things

First, *promise* the deceased that you will do something constructive to bring him peace. It usually means taking care of those he left behind or something he left unfinished.

It never means revenge!

He has risen above revenge in the next world.

Second, *do something* in the name of the deceased. It can be anything, including a donation to charity.

Third, *find peace* yourself.

Understand that the deceased left the earth not in peace but in emotional turmoil. He needs peace. He can see the pain that he has caused to those he left behind but is now powerless to do anything about it. When he looks down and sees you in emotional pain, he cannot have peace either. For his sake and your own sake, it is vital that you get control of your emotions.

Let us pray. We say:

May you have peace where you have gone.

May I have peace, who is left behind.

I forgive you for the pain you caused me.

Please forgive me for the pain I caused you.

Let us both develop from our mistakes.

Perhaps you have now learned that life is valuable.

I also believe that life is valuable.

I shall help someone so that you may have peace.

I shall give to a charity that you may have peace.

I shall pray to God that you may have peace.

To your living children, say the following

Please understand that you cannot control another person's action, only your reaction, whether in failure or rejection. Bad times and failures are not reasons to commit suicide. Neither is a rejection by another.

I hope that you will stay away from drugs and bad company.

I hope you value life and understand that you have come here to develop. You can only do this by passing through the different scenarios that life throws at you.

I hope you know that I deeply love, value, and need you. You should value yourself. You have qualities that are needed in this world.

One has to be strong to exist in this world. However, you can only become strong through control of your emotions and self-discipline.

Find peace yourself

Do not shun work and people. You will get your comfort from them. Keep in touch with your friends. You can be with them without discussing your loss.

If you cannot financially sustain yourself, you will not have peace.

Talk to your therapists, priests, or older and wiser people.

You will also be able to handle your sorrow if you consider this part of your destiny. However, this can be dangerous when you have other children. One should search for the causes of this suicide. If the cause is in the "family dynamics or the family's emotional makeup," then there is a danger of another suicide in the making. An example is an inability to have good relations with others because of poor control of emotions.

Remember that "it is in giving that we receive." By helping others, we are helped. In this case, we receive comfort.

JUDGES, LEADERS, & EMOTIONAL PAIN

CHAPTER 49: SOCIETY & PAIN

Society can bring immense pain to its people or the people of another country. It may attack another country out of hatred or greed for more land and power. We see this happening in Palestine. Our leaders only allow *"selective freedom of speech,"* virtually banning any protest against the immorality of the act.

What happened to the "government by the people?"

But in its own country, the government is capable of immense harm. We have seen it happen when it turned against a section of its people, as in the treatment meted out to the American Indians and in the slavery in the United States. And there was the cruel, unforgivable behavior that was meted out to untouchables in India.

Also cruel was the repression of voting rights for women in the USA until recently.

History has shown that whenever man has an inferiority complex or feels threatened by the ones he thinks are superior to him, he will remove their rights.

But even when, out of so-called "fairness," it applies the laws equally, the government can cause severe emotional harm to its people.

In the present day, immense harm is being done since the government forgets what it should implement and what it should remove.

VERBAL ABUSE

We allow cursing at officials as "freedom of speech," *allowing morale at work to fall.* We do not realize that cursing, demeaning, and insulting is not freedom of speech. **It is verbal abuse and must be punished as severely as physical abuse.**

There is no freedom without responsibility. If you are going to curse, the official should have a right to put a tape on your mouth. Before you cry about your rights, how about starting with your responsibilities towards society and other human beings?

Laws to Prevent Emotional Pain to A Child.

A child's rights are above others, as he is the most helpless of all.

1. No mother should be in the defense forces as long as her child is below 18 years of age.

Otherwise, first, she violates the child's rights to have his mother.

And second, she violates her responsibility to do parenting.

She should not have had a child if she was not willing to do parenting and be with the child. Her career cannot be at the cost of her child's heartache.

2. In cases of divorce, the stability of staying in the same home until adulthood leads to a stable personality of a child.

Which judge would be willing to pick up all his belongings and shift to another house every week?

If the judge cannot handle the strain of this, how dare he put such a burden on a helpless child in the name of fairness to its parents?

The child is shunted back and forth from one parent's house to the other. No one asks what he wants. No one cares what is good for him. The judge does not think once about whether he personally would like to live thus.

The child has no home that is his permanent home. He has no roots. How can he have a stable personality? How can he develop a good character? He is ashamed. He feels inferior. He is at the whims of different parents. He cannot form a strong bond with either parent. They cannot influence his nature.

To hide his pain, he pretends not to care. But beware. You are creating anger, hatred, and non-attachment within him. You, the Judge, are doing this. There are cases of children hurting and killing others. Or, you are creating a child suicide. The harm and pain you are inflicting is unimaginable.

After all, what will hold back a child from doing wrong except his moral map, character, and the desire to please a parent he loves?

He will follow the moral map of a parent if he is given time to imbibe them. But you are not giving him this time.

Even a plant cannot live if you uproot it every week. How did you think of doing this to a human?

Two rules must be followed:

A. **To form a stable personality, a judge must give a child the stability of one place.**

B. Unless she is medically unfit, the child must remain with the mother.

Granted, some men can be good parents, but to talk about equality or fairness is absurd. This is not about fairness to the parent.

This is about the welfare of the child!

The child, his pain, and his personality (that will be affected) must have top priority in this. The child will be a cornerstone of our society tomorrow. He cannot be a pawn in the fight for control by his parents.

God did not make men and women equal in all regards. He gave the uterus and the breasts to the woman for a reason. He made her carry the baby inside her for a reason. Unless the mother is ill, the child must stay with the mother. If God wanted equality, he would have given man a womb.

3. If a parent does not allow the other parent to do parenting, then that must be a reason for divorce.

4. A parent who alienates his child against the other parent and does not give the other parent parenting time with the child must go to jail.

5. A parent who has children and is caught drinking alcohol or taking drugs must go to jail.

Alcohol and drugs impair judgment and lead to child neglect and child abuse. The mother, especially, or a single-parent father, cannot drink alcohol until the child turns eighteen.

The protection of an infant's life and welfare is above the freedom to drink. Our children will determine our future or moral chaos.

It is the duty of the parent to show their children that life can be enjoyed without alcohol or drugs.

6.. "Foster homes" must be banned. They are the cruelest things invented. They causes unimaginable pain to a helpless child as he is shunted from one foster home to another. This is criminal!

He is given no time to bond with an adult figure, develop emotional attachments, and have a set of principles. The idea was created with good intentions to give the child a homelike atmosphere, But it has failed miserably.

Each foster home gives him rejection, non-caring, and different values. He cannot form a stable personality. He does not know how long he will be staying at any place. Could we live this way? Would we do this to someone we love?

Do you know what it is like to have no one love you and no friend of your own, even of your age?

In each home, he is at the mercy of the foster parents, who have very different (or no) ideas of parenting ,anger control or morality.

He is at the mercy of the impulses of the guardians in each foster home, who are often motivated by pure greed. The State cannot possibly keep an eye on each foster home all the time.

This leads to child neglect, child abuse, and severe emotional pain to the child.

Then we wonder why these children have no caring or respect for us. Quite the contrary, they hate us enough to kill us.

If we did not care about their pain, why should they care about ours?

Bring back the orphanages.

To form <u>a stable</u> personality, a judge must give a child the stability of staying in <u>one</u> place.

The stability of "one home" leads to a stable personality.

It is time to admit our mistakes. The orphanages are the best things for the children.

The orphanages are at set places where the State can check on them any time.

The children no longer have the severe anxiety that comes from depending on the whims of the foster parents. And these whims kept changing as the foster parents changed.

Guidelines are placed in the orphanages.

The children stay at the same place until adulthood or adoption. *They form stability instead of fragmentation.* They are at a place where regular classes are held on moral values and character. Self-control and good manners are also be taught.

The children do not fall through the cracks. Each child is accounted for.

Unlike the foster homes, the people working there do not keep changing and, like teachers, can form a deep bond with the child. They become permanent role models.

The children have each other and are not lonely. They can give each other emotional support!

Complaints against the managers who are not doing the job well can be managed without hurting the child.

He does not have to be shunted somewhere else.

Pregnancy

7. It has to be a law that during pregnancy, couples have to go through a course on parenting.

They must attend so many hours of parenting, child punishment, anger management, handling frustration without violence, treating the other parent with respect, sharing finances and chores, self-control, and delaying gratification. These can be found in the author's book on parenting.

8. Common-law marriages must be banned.

During pregnancy, the parents must show a certificate of marriage or risk going to jail. Common-law marriage hurts the child.

The child has a right to a stable and legal home, not one in which anyone can walk out whenever he/she wants. When two people decide to live together, they are acting totally irresponsibly towards each other and their children. They are acting according to their feelings, not responsibilities.

The State cannot afford to handle the fallout from their irresponsibility, the foster homes, the child abuse, and child neglect.

9. If two persons decide to live together, they must not be recognized by the law for any benefits. **Also, their employers must immediately start removing one-third of the salary of each person every month and put it in escrow.** So, if one decides to abscond, the other one will be protected.

10. Any property bought by a living together couple living together without marriage must immediately have a lien on it so that one cannot throw the other person out.

11. A woman who produces one or more children without being able to show that she (not her family) has the means and the inclination to care for them must go to jail for child abuse and child neglect. And she must have her tubes tied.

No freedom can be had at the expense of causing lifelong pain to a minor. Her conduct violates the moral rights of a child to have a parent who is able to take care of her child.

Stop Causing Emotional Pain to a Child!

12. No single mother should be allowed to live alone with her small children to prevent child neglect or child abuse from being overwhelmed.

She must share her home with another parent or be with her parents. She cannot leave her children home alone until they are sixteen.

PARENTING

Lack of parenting must be considered a punishable crime.

Lack of parenting causes emotional pain in the child and, ultimately, in society. Children are not able to grow up normal without parenting.

There is a checklist below that the court can go through, but three things must be asked first.

Do the parents supervise the time spent on social media?

Are the parents aware of who his friends were?

Does the parent understand that a child needs many people as teachers? A child needs many people to reinforce what you teach. These are neighbors, aunts, uncles, grandparents, teachers, principals, police, and other authorities. They can also be total strangers! You must understand that they are helping your child to become a better person! Your child's fear of them can be a strong tool in teaching him self-control.

Do you thank them and agree that your child behaved badly and deserves punishment, thus helping his character to be corrected?

Or do you blindly and angrily attack and complain about the very person who caught your child doing wrong?

Well, then, first, you have just reinforced his wrong behavior!

Second, you have given him no incentive to exercise self-control. Tomorrow, he will want to shoot everyone in the school, and now he has no self-control to stop himself.

You, the parent, should be held responsible and share his punishment.

THE CHECKLIST FOR THE JUDGES: TARP

We start with the acronym "TARP."

T (TARP)

T stands for Time.

T stands for the time a parent spends per day with his child without being on the iPhone, iPad, or computer, whether at home, shopping or at a restaurant. She would rather look at what total strangers say instead of giving her child her attention! If she behaves so, then the court should appoint a social worker to be with her and her child for a week and file a report.

A woman will produce a child and then go to work. Or, she will spend hours at work and would rather be known as a good worker **but will be an "absent parent."**

Why, then, did she have a child? No animal does that, and the animal kingdom does not suffer the pain our society suffers.

A (TARP)

A Stands for Addiction.

A parent gives his child addiction by offering something or by being addicted himself.

1. **The iPad**

An example is getting a child hooked on the iPad or the iPhone for unlimited time when he should not be on it for more than an hour. The selfish parent wants to be left alone. The child must not take his iPhone to school.

Crossing the street while looking at your phone must be made a criminal offense.

2. **Narcotics**

A parent cannot take narcotics or allow others to take narcotics in his house as long as his children are eighteen.

3. **Alcohol**

No parent can take alcohol or other addictive substances until the child has turned eighteen.

He must be sent to jail for doing so. Those who think this only applies to narcotics and not to alcohol are wrong. Alcohol is as addictive and impairs judgment just as much!

It is the duty of the parent to show the child that life can be enjoyed without alcohol.

4. **Watching sexual movies**

Watching sexual movies with a child is a crime and leads the child to addiction.

Did you make sure that your child does not watch movies that depict violence, cruelty, and sex?

5. **Anger is an addiction.**

Did the parent show his child how to manage anger?

6. **Cruelty is an addiction.**

Can the parent show what steps he took to discourage cruelty and encourage kindness?

R (TARP)

R stands for role model.

Has the parent been a good role model in manners, anger management, and self-control? Does he throw things and curse when he is angry? Is his language full of profanity? Does he insult others or show a complete lack of manners?

P (TARP)

P stands for parenting.

PARENTING IS FURTHER DIVIDED INTO THE FOLLOWING.

Note: Only the highlights will be mentioned here.

1. Value of life.

What steps did you take to teach your child to value life?

2. Moral rules

Did you take time to teach him moral rules or ethics from books, your religions, or the author's book? At every step, did you teach him right from wrong?

3. How to speak

Did you teach your child not to shout, curse, demean others,

not to repeat himself more than twice,

not to keep speaking so that the other person cannot get a word in and

not to say, "I do not care!" ?

All of these are verbal abuse, not freedom of speech.

Did you teach your child to speak respectfully to adults? Did you teach him (and yourself) to never say, "I was speaking first," but to say, "Please go ahead?"

Speech and good manners start at home.

4. Anger management

Did you teach him to become absolutely still when he was angry? Did you teach him not to speak when he is angry?

Did you teach him that he cannot hit, throw, or break things when angry?

5. Delay gratification

Did you teach him to delay his gratification? An example is not eating the candy or playing with the toy you just bought until you reach home.

6. Handle frustration without violence

Did you teach him to handle frustration without shouting, attacking, breaking, throwing things, or killing others?

7. Self-discipline

Self-discipline includes sleeping and waking up at fixed times, keeping his room clean and neat, finishing his chores before he plays, and not keeping his iPad or phone in his room or taking it to school. Is your child living according to rules or his whims?

8. Self-control

Self-control means, among other things, control of speech, handling anger and frustration without violence, showing good manners at home, and limiting his time on the iPad and iPhone.

There can be no mental health without self-control and moral values.

9. How to treat others

This includes behavior with family, outsiders, and persons of authority. Did you teach him to treat his elders with respect?

Did you teach that knowledge and wisdom must be respected more than money?

Did you teach him not to bully others, not mock or treat them with anger, contempt, or anger, and to not force yourself upon them?

Did you teach him to share, care, be fair to others, step in if someone is attacked, and defend him?

10. Character

Did you teach him that impulsive behavior will not be tolerated?

Did you teach him right from wrong?

Did you teach him to speak the truth and keep his word?

Did you teach him not to steal?

Did you teach him to fulfill his responsibilities and do the right thing, no matter the price?

Did you teach him always to be fair?

Did you teach him patience? Did you teach him compassion?

Did you teach him to be kind to animals?

Did you teach him self-value and self-respect?

Did you teach him to think for himself and to think before acting?

Did you teach him that cruelty is not a sign of power but the ultimate form of depravity?

Did you teach him that any adult has a right to correct him, and the authorities have a right to punish him if he is caught doing something wrong?

Did you teach him to be accountable? He cannot use "mental health," his past or present circumstances, or PTSD to dodge punishment.

Did you teach him that revenge is never to be used?

He must not obey his friends or superiors when the motive is revenge,

Did you teach him that one does not demand respect from others? One earns it!

Did you teach him that before he talks about his rights, he should mention his duties to others?

Did you teach him to take care of his present and future welfare? Did you teach him to protect himself?

Did you teach him how to handle bad times?

Did you teach him the value of work ethics?

Did you teach him the value of money?

Did you teach him to pray? Did you teach him that all religions should be equally respected as they each lead to God?

One does not insult objects of reverence of another religion.

The foundation of all this has to be laid between 3 and 12 years of age and then continue.

All this must be reviewed with both parents during pregnancy. The parents must complete a course in parenting before the delivery.

Anger management, character training, and parenting courses must be mandatory subjects in high school.

If the child is being punished because of a lack of parenting, as described above, and the crime is not serious, he must be sent to a boarding school of discipline for one year. The parent must either go to jail or attend four weeks of parenting classes (eight hours a day and pass the test).

Lack of parenting and parental irresponsibility must be considered punishable crimes.

When a child is brought to court to receive a sentencing for a crime, his parents must share his punishment for not doing parenting.

COMPANY AND ABUSE

A company should not keep an employee if he has done the following:

Abused or abandoned his child;

Abused or abandoned his spouse and

abused or abandoned his parents.

The government forgets that the purpose of the schools should always be first Moral Rules, then "Character," then "How to Handle Bad Times," and only then, the knowledge of the outside world.

The result is the present moral chaos as children murder their parents, teachers, and other students. No one bothered to teach them to distinguish right from wrong at the age when they could have been reached.

"To educate a man in the mind, but not in morals is to educate a menace to society." President Theodore Roosevelt.

The government has decided that teaching moral laws is the same as teaching "religions" and wants nothing to do with them. It is okay for us to worship the devil freely, but God forbid that we worship our religions and prayers in our schools.

Religion has always emphasized conscience, character, and morals. The reason why pilgrims came here in search of freedom to pray is *that prayer leads to the basis for character.* But now we ban the Ten Commandments being displayed in public out of fear that our children may learn to be good.

Moral laws have nothing to do with religion. They are the same Cosmic laws incorporated by every religion to prevent society from disintegrating into chaos. The following are four important rules:

1. **Moral rules must be taught from kindergarten.**

2. The government must ban teaching of any kind of sexuality in schools and colleges.

The original hope was that if the students learned about sexuality they would refrain from being promiscuous, but quite the opposite has happened! Allowing sexuality to be taught in school is akin to permitting students to indulge in it. Not one positive thing has been attained by doing so.

1. **There have to be rules of decency in our clothing and conduct in public places.**

We have thrown decency out the window and allowed women to be practically nude in public showing their breasts and wearing only G-strings. And then we keep putting a growing number of rapists and child predators in jail. We do not see the connection! ***If one sector will not show self-control, why should the other one?***

When a woman has an inferiority complex, she will hide what she *lacks* in her brain and bring attention to her body. And she will keep pushing the boundary until she is practically nude.

Lack of clothing covers lack of intelligence!

She is deliberately exciting the male. He cannot attack her for various reasons, so he will find a woman weaker than her and rape her. ***And she then becomes morally responsible for this rape.*** She excited him. A chicken cannot say to a lion, "I am going to parade up and down in front of you but you cannot eat me. What do you think the lion will do?

Nature has made laws that man cannot overturn.

GUNS

The public must be banned from having any gun.

When your congressman refuses to do so, he is saying that he does not care if your child or spouse is killed, families are torn apart, and lifelong emotional pain ensues. He does not have the courage to fight for your rights. He is only interested in being popular. So he will come to your funeral and sing your hymns. But he will stop there. He will talk vaguely about the type of guns that should be removed. But all guns can kill!

"The right to have arms" was placed when we, as an infant nation, had no army, no air force, no cars, no police, and no means of instant communication with each other. None of this is valid today.

To insist on an archaic law to please a few people and to ignore the immense suffering and emotional pain it is causing defines non-caring in its extreme.

The End.

END OF SECTION TWO.

M. kukreja, M.D.